SWEET MEMORIES

Desserts From America's Favorite Inns

COMPILED BY LUCILLE BOWLING CARLOFTIS

ISBN: 0-942407-67-9

09 08 07 06 05 / 10 9 8 7 6 5 4 3

FATHER & SON
PUBLISHING, INC.
4909 N. Monroe Street
Tallahassee, Florida 32303
http://fatherson.com
800-741-2712

Special thanks to the Old Rittenhouse Inn, Bayfield, Wisconsin
for the cover illustration

My special thanks to the innkeepers and chefs for
graciously contributing their recipes and preserving
these treasures of America's inns.

Table of Contents

PREFACE

In our travels, my late husband and I grew tired of the same "cookie cutter" structures we found at every exit and began the adventure of searching for unique, often overlooked and out-of-the-way places. The inns and historic bed and breakfasts we found during our travels have graciously shared their favorite dessert recipes with me.

I have combined the best of the memorable recipes from over 130 inns into a valuable resource for entertaining so you readers could share them with family and friends. If you're like me, you probably do not have the time to create such unique and tempting desserts, so I compiled the best selections from across the country into this book of sweet memories.

This book will help you serve your family and guests a lavish variety of delectable dishes from its 245 taste-tested selections while hopefully cultivating your interest in the fascinating array of America's best inns.

Northeast Region

Northeast Region

Sweet Memories

Barnard-Good House

Blueberry Grents

1   egg
⅔   cup flour
2   tablespoons sugar
¼   teaspoon salt
⅓   cup whipping cream
1   teaspoon baking powder

Beat egg with ⅓ cup whipping cream in small bowl. Whisk in flour, sugar, baking powder, and salt. Combine with:

2   tablespoons fresh lemon juice
½   cup water
½   teaspoon freshly grated nutmeg
½   cup sugar
½   teaspoon allspice

Bring to boil, adding:

2   pints fresh or frozen blueberries

Return to boil and reduce to a simmer. Drop in rounded teaspoons of butter, leaving ½ inch between each. Cover and simmer gently for 15-20 minutes. Uncover and test with toothpick.

Barnard-Good House
Built in 1869 and sits in the heart of historic Cape May.

Cape May, New Jersey
238 Perry St. ~ Cape May, NJ 08204 ~ 609-884-5381

Northeast Region

Beekman Arms

Chocolate Bread Pudding

1	tablespoon unsalted butter (for the pan)
2	cups half-and-half
6	ounces semi-sweet chocolate, chopped
1	cup strong black coffee
3	eggs
¼	cup dark rum
¾	cup sugar
1	teaspoon vanilla extract
6	ounces (half a loaf) french bread (1 inch dice)
	Raspberry Sauce and Whipped Cream (for serving)

Butter a 7 x 11-inch baking pan. Heat the half-and-half to a boil. Remove the pan from heat and add the chocolate. Stir until the mixture is smooth. Mix the remaining ingredients (except the bread) together and then mix in slowly the chocolate mixture. Pour the mixture over the bread and allow to sit 30-40 minutes, stirring once or twice.

Preheat the oven to 325 degrees, pour the mixture into the buttered pan and bake for 1 hour, until the pudding is set. Serve warm with a pool of raspberry sauce and a dollop of whipped cream. Raspberry Sauce: puree raspberries, remove seeds. Add sugar if necessary.

Beekman Arms
This is a fabulous repository of our nation's history. Built in 1760, Beekman Arms is America's oldest inn.

Rhinebeck, New York
Route 9 ~ Rhinebeck, NY 12572 ~ 845-876-7077

Sweet Memories   4

Almond Tarte with Fresh Berries

Dough: 1   cup sugar
            2   sticks butter, softened
            2   large eggs
          18   ounces flour
                Pinch of salt

Sift flour into a large mixing bowl. Gradually add softened butter to flour, until the mixture resembles cornmeal. Add sugar, pinch of salt and eggs. Mix thoroughly without overmixing, until the mixture becomes a dough, soft but solid. Pat dough into thick circle; do not overwork. Cover the dough and chill at least 3 hours.

Crème: 2   large eggs
          ½   pound sugar
           1   pound almonds, processed in food processor until a
                fine powder
           4   ounces melted butter

Whisk eggs and sugar together by hand until light and creamy. Add almond powder and melted butter to egg and sugar mixture. Whisk again slowly until all ingredients are blended. Chill almond crème for 2-3 hours.

Continued on page 6

5   *Northeast Region*

Continued from page 5

Tarte: 1   pint fresh raspberries
           1   pint fresh strawberries, halved
           ½   pint fresh blueberries
           ½   kiwi, peeled and sliced into ¼ inch slices
                Orange marmalade

Preheat oven to 375. Remove dough from refrigerator to counter. Roll into large thin circle. Place into tarte pan. Bake shell in oven for 5-10 minutes, just until pastry is lightly browned. Remove from oven; let cool.
Add chilled almond crème to cooled Tarte Shell. Spread crème in even layer to edges of shell. Return filled tarte to oven. Bake for 20 minutes at 375. Remove; let tarte cool completely.
Beginning from the outer edge of tarte shell, place raspberries in a circle on the crème. Place a second circle of blueberries next to the raspberries. Place a third circle of strawberries, cut side down, next to the raspberries. Place another circle of blueberries next to the strawberries. In the center, overlap slices of kiwi so that no almond crème is visible. Heat orange marmalade over low heat until thick and syrupy. Using small pastry brush, brush marmalade over the tarte, being careful to glaze all fruit. Chill tarte for 30 minutes to set glaze. Serves 10.

The Birches Inn
The Birches Inn has contributed to the hospitality of New England for more than 50 years.
New Preston, Connecticut
233 West Shore Road ~ New Preston, CT 06777 ~ 860-868-1735

Maple Walnut Pie

4	eggs, well beaten
⅔	cup sugar
⅛	teaspoon salt
1	cup strong maple syrup
½	cup butter, melted
1	9-inch unbaked pie shell
¾	cup walnuts
1	cup whipping cream

Combine beaten eggs, sugar, salt, maple syrup and add melted butter. Blend.

Pour into pie shell; cover with walnuts. Bake 1 hour at 350 degrees. Test.

Double Berry Cream Cake

1	pint fresh raspberries
1	pint fresh blueberries
¼	cup sugar
3	tablespoons white wine (sweet)
2	cake layers (favorite homemade sponge)
1	pint vanilla ice cream

Mash ½ cup raspberries with sugar and wine; let stand 15 minutes. Add rest of raspberries and blueberries. Place one sponge cake on plate; cover with half of ice cream and half of berry mixture.

Top with remaining cake layer and rest of ice cream and berries.

Northeast Region

Hot Milk Cake

1   cup sugar
2   eggs
1   cup flour
1   teaspoon baking powder
     salt
     vanilla
½   cup boiling milk

Beat eggs and sugar; add flour and baking powder, salt and vanilla. Lastly, add boiling milk gradually. Bake at 350 degrees for 20-30 minutes. Serves 8.

Raw Apple Cake

1½ cups oil
2   cups sugar
3   eggs
3   cups flour
1   teaspoon soda
½   teaspoon salt
1   cup raisins
2   teaspoons vanilla
2   cups apples, chopped
1   cup coconut
1   cup nuts

Mix oil and sugar thoroughly; add all other ingredients. Bake in tube pan at 350 degrees for 1 hour. Make sauce.

Sauce: 1   cup brown sugar
           2-3 tablespoons milk
           ¼   cup butter

Boil 2 minutes. Pour sauce over warm cake.

The Birchwood Inn
An inn for all seasons, this inn can trace its beginnings back to 1775.
Temple, New Hampshire
Route 45 ~ Temple, NH 03084 ~ 603-878-3285

Sweet Memories   8

Blue Harbor House

Bavarian Cream

2   cups milk
6   tablespoons sugar
2   whole eggs
2   egg yolks
2   tablespoons unsalted butter, cut into ½-teaspoon
     pieces
2   tablespoons cornstarch
1   tablespoon vanilla (adjust to taste)

In a medium bowl, mix 3 tablespoons sugar, eggs, egg yolks and corn-starch. In a saucepan, scald milk, 3 tablespoons sugar and vanilla. Slowly stir scalded milk into egg mixture. Return to saucepan. Cook slowly until desired thickness. Remove from heat and return to mixing bowl. Stop cooking by placing mixing bowl into larger bowl with ice and beat until cool, adding butter a little at a time. Add cornstarch to thicken.
Cream will hold for some time in the refrigerator.

Northeast Region

Fruit Napoleon

¼ cup brown sugar
1 tablespoon butter
   Puff pastry sheet
   Bavarian cream
   Sliced almonds
   Powdered sugar
   Egg wash (1 egg yolk, 1 teaspoon water)
   Fresh fruits of the season

Prepare 1 hour before serving. Thaw puff pastry and cut into rectangles, 3-inch by 4-inch. Place pastry on ungreased cookie sheet and brush with egg wash. Sprinkle top of pastry with almonds. Bake at 400 degrees for 10 minutes until pastry is puffed and golden brown. Cool pastry and reserve. Prepare Bavarian cream.

In a saucepan add 1 tablespoon butter, brown sugar and blueberries. Sautee over medium heat until sugar has dissolved and reduce liquid by one half. Add sliced bananas mixing thoroughly, remove from heat and cool.

Cut pastry in half lengthwise to make a sandwich. Spread Bavarian cream over the bottom and place on dish. Spoon sautéed fruit over the Bavarian cream. Spread Bavarian cream on the top half of the pastry and place to make a sandwich. Sprinkle with powdered sugar.

Blue Harbor House
A New England cafe, offering good food and lodging.

Camden, Maine
67 Elm St. ~ Camden, ME 04843 ~ 800-248-3196

The BOW STREET _Inn_

Apple Squares

1¾ cups sugar
3   eggs
2   cups flour
1   teaspoon cinnamon
1   teaspoon baking powder
½   teaspoon salt
1   teaspoon vanilla
1   cup oil
1   cup nuts (chopped)
2   cups apples (peeled and sliced)

Preheat oven to 350 degrees. Mix sugar and eggs together. Mix flour with cinnamon, baking powder and salt. Add these two mixes together. Add oil and vanilla, then nuts and apples. Pour mixture into greased 9 x 11-inch pan. Bake for 45 minutes at 350 degrees.

The Bow Street Inn
The inn's riverside location lends itself admirably to the town's best shops, restaurants and theaters.

Portsmouth, New Hampshire
121 Bow St. ~ Portsmouth, NH 03801 ~ 603-431-7760

Chocolate Terrine

12   ounces semisweet chocolate bits
8   ounces unsalted butter, softened, cut into 4 pieces
½   cup water
1   cup sugar
4   eggs

In food processor, ground chocolate fine. Boil together sugar and water
5 minutes. Turn processor on and pour hot syrup through feed tube to
melt chocolate. Add softened butter a piece at a time. Add eggs. Blend
until smooth. Line a Pyrex leaf pan with buttered wax paper. Pour
batter in. Place in larger pan filled halfway up with hot water and bake
1 hour at 350 degrees. Serve in slices over raspberry puree or coffee
brandy cream sauce.

White Chocolate Coeur A La Crème

1   8-ounce package cream cheese, room temperature
1½   cups whipping cream
¾   cup powdered sugar, sifted
3   ounces white chocolate, melted and slightly cooled
1   12-ounce bag frozen unsweetened raspberries, thawed
⅓   cup sugar
1   8-ounce can unsweetened apricots, drained
     Amaretto liqueur
     Fresh mint leaves

Line six ½-cup coeur a la crème molds with double thickness of dampened cheesecloth, extending enough beyond edges to enclose filling completely. Using electric mixer, beat cream cheese with ¼ cup cream and powdered sugar in large bowl until fluffy. Add chocolate and beat until smooth, about 2 minutes. Whip 1 cup cream to stiff peaks in another bowl. Gently fold into cream cheese mixture. Spoon ½ cup cheese mixture into each prepared mold. Fold cheesecloth over tops. Place molds on rack set over pan. Refrigerate for at least 8 hours or overnight.

Drain raspberries, reserving juice. Puree berries with ⅓ cup sugar in processor. Press through fine sieve into medium bowl to remove seeds. Add just enough reserved juice to thin puree to sauce consistency. Cover and refrigerate. Puree apricots in processor. Add amaretto to taste. Transfer to small bowl. Cover and refrigerate. (Sauces can be prepared 3 hours ahead.) Whip remaining ¼ cup cream to stiff peaks. Spoon into pastry bag fitted with star tip. Pull back cheesecloth and invert 1 mold onto right side of large plate. Carefully remove cheesecloth. Pour 3 tablespoons raspberry sauce on left side of plate. Spoon 1 tablespoon apricot sauce in center of raspberry sauce. Draw knife through center of apricot circle, forming heart pattern. Repeat with remaining molds and sauces. Pipe rosettes of cream onto plate and garnish with mint leaves. Makes 6 servings.

13   *Northeast Region*

Truffle Tarte

Pastry:	6	tablespoons chilled unsalted butter
	1	egg yolk
	1	pinch salt
	1	cup flour
	3	tablespoons cocoa powder
	3	tablespoons sugar

Process in Cuisinart till crumbled fine. With machine on, add 3 tablespoons ice water and process till large lump of dough forms.
Roll out on floured board. Line pastry pan with removable base with pastry. Line with wax paper and rice and bake for 6 minutes at 400 degrees. Remove rice and bake 3 minutes more. Set aside.

Filling:	1	cup sugar
	3	eggs
	¼	cup cocoa powder
	1	cup light cream
	3	tablespoons Chamborde liqueur

Process till smooth. Pour into prepared crust and bake 400 degrees until set, about 30 minutes. Cool thoroughly.

Fudge:	2	cups chocolate bits
	1½	sticks softened unsalted butter
	3	tablespoons Chamborde
	3	egg yolks (dip raw eggs in boiling water 30 seconds to kill any bacteria on shell)
	⅓	cup boiling water

Grind chocolate in Cuisinart till fine. With machine on, pour in enough water to melt chocolate thoroughly. Add egg yolks, butter and Chamborde. Divide mixture in half. Spread half mixture onto cooled tarte.

The Bramble Inn
This very charming inn is located in the heart of Cape Cod's historic district.

Brewster, Cape Cod, Massachusetts
Route 6A ~ P.O. Box 807 ~ Brewster, MA 02631 ~ 508-896-7644

The Brass Heart Inn

Peaches and Cream Pie

2	egg yolks
2	tablespoons flour
⅔	cup sugar
¼	teaspoon almond extract
⅓	cup melted butter
4-5	fresh peaches peeled and halved
1	unbaked pie shell

Combine and blend first 5 ingredients. Place peach halves cut side up in pie shell, pour custard mixture over peaches. Bake 15 minutes at 400 degrees then turn oven to 300 degrees and bake another 20 to 30 minutes.

This is best served at room temperature. Fresh raspberries or apricots are good fruits for this pie also.

Maple Frango

    3   large egg yolks
    ½   cup pure maple syrup, boiling hot
    2   cups heavy cream

Beat the egg yolks until they are thick and very light in color. Heat maple syrup to boiling and slowly pour into beaten egg yolks, beating constantly. Let cool. Whip heavy cream until stiff, and fold into cooled maple custard. Freeze until firm and serve.

The Brass Heart Inn

Surrounded by acres of rolling fields with Mt. Chocorua as a backdrop, this rambling structure dates back to 1778.

Chocorua, New Hampshire

88 Philbrick Neighborhood Rd. ~ P.O.Box 270 ~ Chocorua, NH 03817 ~ 603-323-7766

Bourbon Pecan Pie

1	9-inch pie crust
3	eggs
1	cup dark corn syrup
1	cup granulated sugar
1	teaspoon vanilla extract
2	teaspoons melted butter
1	ounce bourbon
1¼	cups pecan halves

Beat eggs, corn syrup and sugar until smooth. Add vanilla and butter, whip thoroughly. Stir in bourbon and pecans. Pour into pie shell. Bake at 350 degrees for 45-50 minutes, or until tests done with knife.

The Cameron Estate Inn
Is one of Pennsylvania's most elegant inns that dates back to 1805.

Mount Joy, Pennsylvania
Box 305 ~ Mount Joy, PA 17552 ~ 717-653-1773

The Captain Lord Mansion

Pumpkin Spice Bars

4	eggs
2	cups sugar
1	cup vegetable oil
1	can pumpkin
2	cups flour
2	teaspoons baking powder
2	teaspoons cinnamon
1	teaspoon baking soda
¾	teasponn salt
½	teaspoon ginger
¼	teaspoon ground cloves
½	cup raisins

Heat oven to 350 degrees. Grease 15½ x 10½ x 1-inch pan. Beat eggs, sugar, oil and pumpkin. Stir in remaining ingredients, and pour into pan. Bake for 25-30 minutes. Cool and frost with cream sheese frosting.

Cream cheese frosting:
Mix 3 ounces of softened cream cheese, 4 cup plus 2 tablespoons softened margarine or butter and 1 teaspoon vanilla. Gradually beat in 2 cups of powdered sugar until frosting is smooth and of spreading consistency.

Whoopie Pies

6	tablespoons Crisco
1	cup sugar
1	egg
1	teaspoon vanilla
1	cup milk
5	tablespoons cocoa
2	cups flour
1¼	teaspoons baking soda
1	teaspoon salt

Cream together Crisco, sugar and egg. Then add vanilla and milk. Mix well. Add dry ingredients and mix well. Drop by spoonfulls onto ungreased cookie sheet. Bake at 350 degrees for 10-12 minutes. Let cool completely before sandwiching them onto cream mixture.

Cream mixture:

⅔	cup Crisco
½	cup sugar
1	tablespoon water
1	teaspoon vanilla
½	cup evaporated milk

Place all ingredients in bowl and mix at high speed for 10 minutes.

The Captain Lord Mansion
One of the most romantic Kennebunkport bed and breakfast inns on the Southern Maine Coast. Romance is evident in all the details and special touches found in the luxurious guestrooms.

Kennebunkport, Maine
P.O. Box 800 ~ Kennebunkport, ME 04046 ~ 800-522-3141

Chocolate Marble Cheesecake

Crust: 3 cups graham cracker crumbs
1 cup sugar
1 cup melted butter

Mix ingredients together and put into a 9-inch springform pan.

Filling: 3 8-ounce packages cream cheese
1 cup sugar
1 cup heavy cream
3 eggs
2 tablespoons vanilla
2 ounces unsweetened Baker's chocolate

Blend cream cheese and sugar together. Add eggs, vanilla and heavy cream. Mix well. In a double boiler, melt chocolate. Take off heat and mix in one cup of filling. Pour remaining filling into crust. Swirl in chocolate mixture. Bake in oven at 350 degrees for 1 hour.

Sweet Memories   20

Blueberry Cheesecake

Make the cheesecake filling the same as for the chocolate marble cheesecake, except leave out the chocolate. Bake at 350 degrees for 1 hour.

Topping: 3   cups fresh blueberries, divided
                2   cups sugar

Take 1 cup blueberries and mash down and cook in heavy pot. Boil for five minutes continually stirring. Then add sugar and cook down until it thickens to a jelly consistency. Stir in 2 more cups of fresh blueberries. Let cool and spread on cheesecake after plain cheesecake has been cooked and cooled.

Fern Hall

This rambling stone mansion was the home of James Wood Johnson, one of the founders of Johnson and Johnson Pharmaceutical Co.

Carbondale, Pennsylvania
Route 247 ~ Carbondale, PA 18407 ~ 570-222-3676

Fitzwilliam Inn

Ice Cream Ball

3	cups corn flakes, slightly crushed
1	cup chopped walnuts
1	cup brown sugar
1	cup coconut
½	cup melted butter

Combine all ingredients. Roll large scoop of ice cream in mixture and serve with favorite sauce.

Fitzwilliam Inn
This noted hostelry has had a reputation for serving fine food since 1796.
Fitzwilliam, New Hampshire
62 Route 119 West ~ Fitzwilliam, NH 03461 ~ 603-585-3400

Five Gables Inn

Baked Apples in Puff Pastry

8	apples or pears, peeled and cored
½	cup sugar
2	tablespoons cinnamon
½	cup butter cut into ½-inch cubes
2	prepared puff pastry sheets
1	egg, beaten with 1 teaspoon water
¼	cup brown sugar

Mix together sugar, cinnamon and butter. Fill the centers of the apple with the mixture. Sprinkle a little of the sugar and cinnamon over the apples.

Lightly roll out the puff pastry and cut into 5-6 inch squares, large enough to enclose an apple. Place apple in center of pastry square and pull up edges of pastry to enclose the apple. Pinch the edges to seal. Brush the pastry with the egg and water wash.

Arrange on baking sheet lined with parchment paper. Bake at 375 degrees for 25-30 minutes. Dust with brown sugar.

Irresistible Cookies

2	cups butter
2	cups brown sugar
2	cups white sugar
4	eggs
2	teaspoons vanilla
4	cups flour
2	teaspoons baking powder
2	teaspoons baking soda
2	cups chocolate chips
3	cups raisins
3	cups nuts
2	cups old-fashioned rolled oats
2	teaspoons salt

Blend the butter with the two sugars until creamy. Add the eggs and vanilla, beat until well mixed. Sift flour, baking powder, salt and baking soda. Add to egg mixture, beat well. Stir in remaining ingredients. When well mixed, stir into golf ball size and bake on ungreased cookie sheet at 375 degrees for 8-10 minutes or until barely golden. Best when slightly undercooked and warm from the oven. Dough keeps well when refrigerated, or make dough into balls and freeze in freezer bags until ready to bake. Bake as needed. Makes 200.

Blueberry or Apple Crisp

3		cups blueberries (fresh or frozen) or enough peeled, cored and sliced apples to fill the pie plate

Topping:	½	cup brown sugar
	½	cup sugar
	¼	teaspoon nutmeg
	½	teaspoon cinnamon
	¾	cup flour
	½	cup butter
	1	cup old-fashioned oats, uncooked

Place blueberries or apples in shallow baking dish. Sift dry ingredients and cut in butter. Add oats and mix well. Grease a 9-inch pie dish and fill with blueberries. Sprinkle topping evenly over fruit. Bake at 350 degrees for about 30 minutes or until topping is crisp.

Can be assembled the night before and kept covered in the refrigerator until baking.

NOTE: if apples are used, you can mix them with some raisins. But don't let the raisins show above the topping or they will burn.

Pumpkin-Cranberry Bread Pudding with a B&B and Vanilla Custard Sauce

Pudding:	4	cups milk
	4	eggs
	2	egg yolks
	16	ounces canned pumpkin puree
	½	cup sugar
	1½	teaspoons cinnamon
	½	teaspoon nutmeg
	½	teaspoon ground cloves
	½	teaspoon ground ginger
	¾	pound of whole wheat bread cut in ½-inch cubes
	2	cups cranberries, fresh or frozen
	1	cup & a dash B&B Liqueur or Brandy/Bourbon

Combine all pudding ingredients. Spoon into a greased 9 x 13 baking pan. Bake at 350 degrees for 1 hour.

Sauce:	2	cups half and half
	6	egg yolks
	¾	cup sugar
	1	teaspoon vanilla extract

Bring half and half just to a simmer in a saucepan. Combine yolks and sugar in a heat proof bowl. Add a very small amount of half and half to the yolks and sugar, beating constantly with a wire whisk. Pour mixture back into sauce pan with remaining half and half, still beating with the whisk. Place over medium heat and stir constantly until thickened and can coat the back of a spoon. DO NOT BOIL. Stir in vanilla extract. Keep warm until ready to serve with the pudding.

Spoon cooked bread pudding into an attractive serving dish. Ladle some custard sauce over the top. Serve the rest of the sauce on the side.

Five Gables Inn

Offering spectacular views of Linikin Bay and it is Boothbay's only summer hotel.

East Boothbay, Maine

P.O. Box 335 ~ Murray Hill Road ~ East Boothbay, ME 04544-0335 ~ 800-451-5048

The Frenchtown Inn

Maple Pecan Tart

1½ cups heavy cream
¾   cup sugar
¾   cup maple sugar
2   whole eggs
2   teaspoons vanilla extract
2   cups pecans
1   teaspoon grated orange rind
    unbaked tart shell

Place your heavy cream and sugar in a saucepan and simmer for approximately 25 minutes, whisking constantly until it thickens to coat the back of a spoon. Let cool slightly.

Add the maple syrup and orange zest to the cream mixture. In a separate bowl whisk the eggs and vanilla together, then add the cool maple syrup mixture. Whisk thoroughly to incorporate.

Preheat oven to 350 degrees. Add the 2 cups of pecans to the unbaked tart shell and pour the maple syrup mixture over and bake approximately 25-30 minutes until set. Cool and cut when ready to serve.

Makes 10 individual 2½-inch tart shells or 2 9-inch tart shells.

Northeast Region

Butternut Squash Pie

2½	cups squash puree
⅔	cup brown sugar
⅓	cup honey or molasses
1	teaspoon ground ginger
½	teaspoon cinnamon
½	teaspoon allspice
¼	teaspoon nutmeg
½	teaspoon salt
1	cup heavy cream
3	eggs
1	teaspoon flour
Crust:	2	cups flour
	8	ounces butter
	½	teaspoon salt
	1	cup ground walnuts
	½	cup sugar
	1	egg yolk
	2½	ounces orange juice
	½	teaspoon orange rind (optional)

Mix in a bowl the squash puree, brown sugar, honey, ground ginger, cinnamon, allspice, nutmeg and salt. Whisk together the heavy cream, eggs and flour, then add to the other mixture. Bake 15 minutes at 425 degrees then 30-40 minutes at 325 degrees.

The Frenchtown Inn
Built on the Delaware River in 1838, this handsome old structure is dedicated to excellence and first class service.

Frenchtown, New Jersey
7 Bridge Street ~ Frenchtown, NJ 08825 ~ 908-996-3300

The Golden Stage Inn

Stage Puffs

1	cup water
1	cup flour
¼	pound butter
4	beaten eggs

Boil water and butter. At once add flour, mixing over low heat until mixture clings together. Slowly add eggs, blending well. Drop by large tablespoon onto cookie sheet, or use a pastry bag for more decorative puffs. Bake 30 minutes at 400 degrees.

Filling:	2	8-ounce packages soft cream cheese
	1	cup confectioner's sugar
	½	cup heavy cream
	3	drops cinnamon oil
	½	cup mini chocolate chips
	½	orange rind grated

In processor mix cream cheese, sugar, and cream until smooth, then mix in remainder of ingredients. Chill until firm. Fill each puff. Drizzle with chocolate fudge sauce or dust with powdered sugar. Can be frozen for up to 2 weeks.

The Golden Stage Inn

This charming inn has a long colorful history. A stagecoach stop and link in the Underground Railroad.

Proctorsville, Vermont

399 Depot Street ~ P.O. Box 218 ~ Proctorsville, VT 05153-0218 ~ 800-253-8226

Northeast Region

Governor's Inn

Apricot Victorian

1   one pound can apricot halves (drained)
¼   cup lemon juice
1   one pound jar apricot jam

Purée apricots. Add lemon juice. Melt down apricot jam, Strain out solids, add liquid apricot to purée mixture. Freeze. When ready to serve, using a round ice cream scoop, place a scoop in a footed glass compote and cover with 1½ ounces of heavy cream.

Old Fashioned Sponge Cake

4   egg yolks, well beaten. Add:
1½   cups sugar. Beat well, and add:
½   cup cold water. Add:
1½   cups sifted all-purpose flour
1½   teaspoons baking powder
      pinch of salt
1   teaspoon pure vanilla extract

Beat egg whites until stiff. Fold in other ingredients. Add vanilla extract. Pour into a 10-inch prepared tube pan. Bake in 350 degree oven for 50 minutes (more or less, depending on your oven). Cool in the pan. Slice with a bread knife.

Bourbon Balls

3   boxes vanilla wafers, finely ground
1½ cups bourbon
3   cups chopped nuts
6   tablespoons dry cocoa powder
4½ tablespoons white Karo syrup

Mix bourbon and syrup. Add wafers, nuts and cocoa. Roll teaspoon sized balls and roll in granulated sugar. Rest each in a petit four paper. Store in refrigerator until ready to serve. Will keep indefinitely.

Cranberry Sorbet with Lime

1   one pound can whole berry cranberry sauce
1   small container frozen limeade
¾   cup champagne or still white wine (it is also fun to substitute red wine for a completely different taste treat)
2   egg whites

Place all ingredients in a food processor and buzz until completely blended. Pour into a metal cake pan and freeze until almost solid. Return to food processor and whip until frothy. Pour into a plastic freezer container and store until ready to use. Scoop into a beautiful footed compote and splash liberally with champagne. Serve at once garnished with a wheel of lime and parsley. Will serve 12 or more.

Northeast Region

Pink Grapefruit Sorbet

2   cans grapefruit sections
¼   cup vermouth
2   tablespoons grenadine
½   cup simple syrup*
4   egg whites
½   cup reserved grapefruit juice

Drain grapefruit, reserve juice. Place drained fruit in work bowl of food processor and with the metal blade in place pulse 5 or 6 times. Add remaining ingredients. Pulse to blend. Freeze in an ice cream maker according to manufacturer's directions.
*Consult your favorite instructional cookbook.

Chocolate Mousse Pie

1   package semi sweet chocolate (8 squares)
¼   cup water
8   eggs, separated
1½   teaspoons pure vanilla extract
⅔   cup sugar

Melt chocolate with water in a double boiler, stirring until smooth. Stir in egg yolks and add vanilla. Place chocolate in large bowl. Beat egg whites in large mixer until foamy. Gradually beat in sugar until stiff peaks form, about three minutes. Stir a small amount into chocolate mixture to lighten; fold chocolate and remaining whites together.
Pour four cups into a buttered 9-inch pie pan sprinkled with sugar. Chill remaining mixture. Bake at 350 degrees for 25 minutes or until just set. Cool slightly, then chill one hour. Center will fall forming shell. Spoon remaining chilled mixture into chilled shell. Refrigerate overnight or at least three hours. When ready to serve, slice and garnish with freshly whipped heavy cream. Sprinkle liberally with nutmeg.

The Governor's Inn Tea Dates

1   pound pitted dates
1   cup chopped almonds
    sugar
2   teaspoons sweet unsalted butter
1   tablespoon honey

Stuff the dates with the chopped nuts and roll lightly in sugar. Using a very small heavy bottomed sauce pan, melt the butter and combine with the honey and gently bring to a boil. "Fry" the dates in the mixture. Roll hot dates in sugar and serve at once.

Governor's Inn
Judged one of the nation's ten best, this inn provides the kind of warm welcome, good food and lodging one would expect to find in a New England inn.

Ludlow, Vermont
86 Main Street ~ Ludlow, VT 05149 ~ 800-468-3766

Raspberry Cheese Pie

¼   cup sugar
1¼ cups boiling water
1   cup heavy whipped cream
⅓   cup confectioners sugar
4   ounces raspberry gelatin
1   tablespoon fresh lemon juice
10 ounces frozen raspberries
4   ounces softened cream cheese
1   teaspoon vanilla
1   9-inch pie shell, baked
    dash salt

Red layers: Dissolve gelatin and granulated sugar in boiling water. Add frozen berries and lemon juice and stir until berries set. Chill until partially set.

White layers: Blend cheese, confectioners sugar, vanilla and salt. Fold in whipped cream. Spread half of white mixture on cooled, baked 9-inch pie shell. Cover with half of red mixture and repeat process. Chill until set.

Greenville Arms
Built in 1889, this inn is ideally located near the Hudson River and northern Catskills.

Greenville, New York
Rt. 32 South Street ~ PO Box 659, Greenville, NY 12083 ~ 888-665-0044

Hickory Bridge Farm

Aunt Lillian's Delicious Cookies

1   cup white sugar
1   cup brown sugar
1   cup margarine
1   egg
1   cup oil
1   teaspoon vanilla
1   teaspoon salt
1   teaspoon cream of tartar
1   teaspoon baking soda
1   cup rice krispies
1   cup coconut
1   cup oatmeal
3½ cups flour

Cream shortening and sugar. Add egg. Then add all the other ingredients and mix. Drop by spoonfuls on greased cookie sheet, press with fork. Bake 10-12 minutes at 350 degrees. These cookies keep well in cookie can.

Shoo Fly Pie (gooey bottom)

Topping: 1   cup flour
               ½   cup light brown sugar
               ¼   cup shortening

Mix ingredients together, using a pastry blender, until very fine. Set aside.

Filling: 1   cup boiling water
               1   cup light molasses
               1   teaspoon baking soda
               1   egg

Add water to molasses, then soda. Add egg and pour crust-deep into unbaked 10-inch pie pan. Using a large spoon, mix the crumb mixture well into the molasses filling. Bake in moderate oven at 325 degrees for 35-40 minutes.

Hickory Bridge Farm

This clapboard structure has the homey look it was meant to have amidst tall shade trees, farm implements and an old rail fence.

Orrtanna, Pennsylvania
96 Hickory Bridge Rd. ~ Orrtanna, PA 17353 ~ 717-642-5261

The Holloway House

Old Time Lemon Pie

3	1-inch slices of day-old bread, crusts removed
1	cup boiling water
1	cup sugar
2	eggs, separated
1	lemon, juiced with the rind grated
¼	teaspoon salt

Butter bread and place in a mixing bowl. Pour boiling water over it, and allow to cool. Add sugar, beaten egg yolks, lemon juice and rind and salt. Mix together, and fold in egg whites, stiffly beaten. Pour into an unbaked pie shell and bake at 350 degrees for approximately 30 minutes.

French Chocolate Pie

¾	cup sugar
½	cup butter
1	ounce unsweetened chocolate, melted and cooled
2	eggs
1	teaspoon vanilla

Cream butter. Add sugar and beat until light and fluffy. Add melted chocolate and vanilla and beat well. Add eggs, one at a time, beating for five minutes after adding each egg. Spread in baked 8-inch pie shell. Serve with a dollop of whipped cream. Keep refrigerated.

Southern Peanut Cream Pie

1	baked pie shell
1	cup confectioner's sugar
½	cup smooth peanut butter
¼	cup cornstarch
⅔	cup sugar
¼	teaspoon salt
2	cups milk (scalded)
3	egg yolks, beaten
¼	teaspoon vanilla
3	tablespoons butter
3	egg whites
6	tablespoons sugar for meringue

Combine confectioner's sugar and peanut butter, blend until it appears like biscuit mix. Spread half of mixture on baked pie shell. Now combine cornstarch, sugar and salt. Add scalded milk and mix well. Pour small amount over beaten egg yolks and mix well, then return all to milk mixture. Cook in top of double boiler until mixture thickens. Add butter and vanilla. Cool. Pour into pie shell and top with meringue and sprinkle remainder of peanut butter/sugar mix on top. Bake 325 degrees until meringue browns.

The Holloway House
This inn has offered the same fine food to travellers since 1808

East Bloomfield, New York
Routes 5 & 20 ~ PO Box 26 ~ East Bloomfield, NY 14443-0026 ~ 585-657-7120

The Homestead Inn

Rice Dessert

½   pound rice
4   cups whipping cream
2   cups half and half

Simmer until rice is tender. Then temper hot milk with:

6   egg yolks
½   pound sugar
1   cup whipping cream

Add 1 cup raisins. Sprinkle with cinnamon. Bake at 350 degrees in a water bath till set about 1 hour.

Turtle Cheesecake

Crust: 2   cups crushed pecans
           ½   cup sugar
           ½   cup melted butter

Press into 10-inch pan. Unwrap Kraft® caramels and place on top of crust.

Filling: 1½ pounds cream cheese
          1   cup sugar
          6   eggs

Mix till smooth and add ½ cup cocoa. Pour over crust. Cover pan with tinfoil and bake at 350 degrees in a water bath. Cook about 1 hour or until you see it puff up with hairline cracks. Cool for about 4 hours.

Topping:
         ½   **cup whipped cream, heated until it begins to steam**
       1½ **cups chocolate chips**

Pour over cheesecake. Place whole pecans for servings markings. Let topping cool.

Bread Pudding

  12 slices stale bread
   1 cup sugar
   6 cups scalded milk
   ½ teaspoon cinnamon
   4 tablespoons butter
   6 eggs, beaten
   ½ teaspoon salt
   1 cup moist raisins

Toast bread lightly and spread with butter while hot. Break into buttered 14 x 10 x 2-inch baking pan. Stir the salt and all but 3 teaspoons of sugar into beaten eggs, adding milk and stirring. Pour over bread and let stand 10 minutes, then stir in raisins. Mix 3 tablespoons sugar with cinnamon and sprinkle over the top. Bake at 350 degrees for approximately 45 minutes. Serves 12.

Caramel Cashew Cheesecake

Crust: 2   cups graham crackers ground
½   cup sugar
½   cup melted butter

Filling: 1½   pounds cream cheese
1   cup sugar
6   eggs

Mix crust ingredients and press into 10 inch springform pan. Mix cheesecake ingredients, add 1 tablespoon vanilla. Add cup unsalted cashews on top of crust with Kraft caramels (about 15 caramels). Pour cheesecake on top. Bake in water bath with pan wrapped in tinfoil for about 1 hour. Cool for about 4 hours. Top with whipped cream reversed shell borders.

The Homestead Inn
Meals are graciously served, offering the very best in country cooking since 1762.

Walpole, New Hampshire
Turnpike St ~ Walpole, NH 03608 ~ 603-756-3320

THE HOTEL HERSHEY

Supreme Chocolate Almond Torte

Cream:
2½	cups unsalted butter
4	cups confectioner's sugar
1½	cups vegetable shortening
1	cup cream fondant
1½	teaspoons vanilla extract
8	ounces Hershey's semisweet chocolate chips, melted
2-3	ounces warm water

In a large mixer bowl, beat butter and sugar well. Add shortening, fondant and vanilla extract. Beat until creamy and very smooth. Add chocolate and water, if desired, to adjust consistency. Makes 3 pounds.

Glaze:
8	ounces Hershey's semisweet chocolate chips
½	cup unsalted butter

Melt together chips and butter. Blend until smooth. Makes 1½ cups.

Torte:	1¼	cups butter
	1¾	cups sugar
	4	eggs
	1½	teaspoons vanilla extract
		dash salt
	2¼	ounces Hershey's Premium European Style Cocoa
	½	cup plus 1 tablespoon flour
	4	ounces ground toasted almonds

Heat oven to 350 degrees. In a large mixing bowl, beat together butter and sugar until creamy. Add eggs, one at a time, until well blended. Add vanilla and salt. Sift together cocoa and flour. Beat into the butter mixture. Stir in almonds.

Pour into a 10-inch cake pan. Bake 45 minutes or until a wooden pick inserted in center comes out clean. Remove cake from pan. Cool thoroughly. Frost with Cream. Glaze.

Chocolate Mousse

8	ounces Hershey's semisweet chocolate, chopped
1½	ounces Hershey's unsweetened baking chocolate, chopped
¼	cup warm water
2	tablespoons Kirschwasser
5	eggs, separated
½	cup granulated sugar, divided
1	pint heavy cream
	Chocolate shavings, for garnish

In bowl over warm water, melt chocolate. Stir warm water and Kirschwasser into melted chocolate. In mixer bowl, beat egg yolks and ¼ cup sugar until thickened. Fold into chocolate mixture. In separate bowl, beat egg whites until foamy. Gradually beat in remaining ¼ cup sugar until soft peaks form. Fold into chocolate mixture.

Fill champagne or wine glasses with chocolate mousse. Garnish with chocolate shavings. Serves 12.

Chocolate Cheesecake

3¾ pounds cream cheese
2⅔ cups sugar
8 eggs
1 pound, 4 ounces Hershey's semisweet chocolate
   chips, melted
¼ cup Kahlua
1 quart plus 3½ cups heavy cream
   Chocolate cookie crumbs or graham cracker crumbs

Heat oven to 300 degrees. In a large bowl, beat together cream cheese and sugar until smooth. Add eggs, one at a time, blending well after each addition. Blend until smooth. Add melted chocolate. Blend well. Add Kahlua. Gradually add heavy cream, blending well. Cover bottom of 3 10-inch springform cake pans with chocolate or graham cracker crumbs. Fill each pan with batter, dividing evenly. Bake in water bath for 1 hour. Makes 3 10-inch cakes.

Chocolate Sabayon Cake

¾ cup egg yolks
½ cup sugar
⅔ ounce (3 packets) gelatin
⅔ cup water
8 ounces Hershey's semisweet chocolate chips
¾ cup plus 2 tablespoons sherry
3 cups heavy cream
   Confectioners' sugar
   Vanilla extract to taste
2 10-inch chocolate cake layers (recipe attached)
   Chocolate Buttercream (recipe attached)
   Chocolate shavings

In a large bowl over warm water, whip egg yolks and sugar until thick and lemon-colored.
In small bowl, combine gelatin and water. Let stand until gelatin is dissolved. In top of double boiler over hot boiling water, melt chocolate chips. Stir in sherry and gelatin mixture until smooth. Stir in egg yolk mixture.

In large mixer bowl, beat heavy cream and sugar until soft peaks form. Add vanilla to taste. Fold into chocolate mixture.

Place 1 cake layer in bottom of 10-inch pan or ring. Fill with chocolate sabayon. Top with second cake layer. Refrigerate until firm, or freeze. Just before serving, frost cake with Chocolate Buttercream and coat with chocolate shavings.

Chocolate Cake (for Sabayon Cake)

2 cups cake flour
2 teaspoons baking powder
½ teaspoon baking soda
¼ teaspoon salt
⅔ cups cocoa
1½ cups sugar
½ cup plus 2 tablespoons vegetable shortening
½ cup water
⅔ cup milk
2 eggs
1½ teaspoons vanilla extract

Preheat oven to 350 degrees. Sift together flour, baking powder, baking soda, salt, cocoa and sugar. Add shortening, water, milk, eggs and vanilla. Use electric mixer and slowly blend until ingredients are mixed. Mix about 3 minutes at medium speed, frequently scraping the bowl.

Pour mixture evenly into 2 greased and floured 9-inch cake pans. Bake 25 to 30 minutes, until the top springs back when pressed. Cool in pan 8 to 10 minutes, then invert on racks and remove pans to finish cooling. Makes 2 9-inch layer cakes.

The Hotel Hershey
The Hotel Hershey has provided elegance and warm hospitality since 1933 and its streetlights are shaped like Hershey Kisses.

Hershey, Pennsylvania
100 Hotel Rd. ~ Hershey, PA 17033 ~ 717-533-2171

Northeast Region

The Inn at Castle Hill

Tarte Linzer (Raspberry Nut Tart)

1   cup all-purpose flour
½   cup granulated sugar
½   pound unsalted butter
2   egg yolks
1   cup raspberry preserves
    vanilla extract to taste
1   cup chopped toasted hazelnuts
½   cup toasted chopped almonds
    pinch salt, cinnamon, ground cloves, baking powder

Toast all nuts slightly and let cool at room temperature. Whip egg yolks until fluffy, combining the sugar slowly. Mix butter until soft and smooth and add all sifted dry ingredients (flour, spices). Combine the nuts with the dough and then finish by adding the egg and sugar mixture to nutty dough. Line bottom of springform pan with approximately ⅔ of dough. Place preserves in center of dough and spread evenly, leaving a ½-inch border around the edges. With remaining dough roll out pencil-size strips and form lattice or simple cross pattern on top. Bake at 350 degrees ½ hour or until top browns.

The Inn at Castle Hill
With views of Newport Harbor, this inn has entertained notables such as Thornton Wilder.

Newport, Rhode Island
590 Ocean Dr. ~ Newport, RI 02840 ~ 401-849-3800

Chocolate Pudding Cake

2½ cups flour
½   cup unsweetened cocoa powder
2   teaspoons cinnamon
2½ cups sugar
2   tablespoons baking powder
2   pinches salt
4   ounces bittersweet chocolate, cut up
1½ sticks (12 tablespoons) sweet butter
2   teaspoons vanilla
2   cups whole milk, warmed
3½ cups strong black coffee with flavored liqueurs if
    desired (try bourbon, frangelica, etc.)

Combine first 6 ingredients in mixing bowl. In double boiler, melt chocolate and butter over hot, not boiling, water. Top pan should not touch water. Remove pan from heat and stir in vanilla and milk. Pour chocolate mixture into dry ingredients and stir with wooden spoon to combine.
Set the oven at 350 degrees. Butter a large baking dish (casserole) or individual ramekins and place in refrigerator to set the butter.
Transfer the batter to the baking dish or ramekins and set on half sheet pans. Pour the coffee into the batter. DO NOT STIR. Bake 45 to 55 minutes or until a crust forms on top. The bottom will be puddinglike. Serves 12.

Northeast Region

Apple and Raisin-Filled Shortcakes
with Applejack Cream

Filling: 3½ pounds golden delicious apples, peeled, cored and
                sliced ⅓-inch thick
            4½ tablespoons lemon juice
            4   ounces butter
            1½ cups superfine sugar
            ¾   teaspoon ground cinnamon
            ¼   teaspoon grated nutmeg
            ¾   cup golden raisins
            ½   cup Applejack

Keep sliced apples in cold water with one tablespoon lemon juice to prevent them from browning. Melt butter over medium heat. Stir in sugar, three tablespoons lemon juice and spices. Drain apples and add, along with the raisins. Stir to coat. Cover. Cook until tender (10-15 minutes). Uncover. Remove from heat. Pour liqueur into corner of pan and heat briefly until it ignites. Shake pan until flame subsides. Remove apples and raisins with a slotted spoon. Boil until syrup is reduced by half and starts to caramelize. Add apples.
This can be made in advance, refrigerated and rewarmed for serving.

Shortcake: 1½ cups unbleached all-purpose flour
             2½ teaspoons baking powder
             1   tablespoon sugar
             4   ounces butter, chilled and cut into ¼-inch cubes
             1   tablespoon chilled shortening
             ¾   cup half and half
             2   tablespoons melted butter
                 pinch of salt

Preheat oven to 425 degrees. Lightly grease a baking sheet. Blend flour, baking powder, sugar and salt in a food processor. Blend in butter and shortening using on/off technique until you have a coarse meal. Slowly add half and half. Turn off processor immediately.
Flour your hands and work surface. Gather dough into a ball and roll out to approximately ¼-inch thick. Cut out 12 rounds using a 3-inch cutter with flour as needed (reroll dough if necessary). Brush circles of dough with melted butter and arrange on a baking sheet. Bake until brown, about 15-18 minutes.

Cream: 1   cup whipped cream
         2   tablespoons confectioner's sugar
         1   tablespoon applejack liqueur

Whip the cream with sugar to soft peaks. Fold in Applejack.
Split biscuits and lightly butter each half. Divide half the apple mixture and spread onto half of the biscuits. Top each of these with the other half of the biscuit. Spoon over the rest of the apple mixture and top with whipped cream and a sprinkle of cinnamon.

Fresh Fruit Galette

¼   teaspoon salt
1   cup flour
¼   cup cornmeal
7   tablespoons butter
½   cup sour cream
     iced water

In the processor, blend on/off method. With processor running add butter, sour cream and some ice water.
Roll out dough in circle. Fill with pears in lemon or lime juice, cranberries, any fruit or savory topping. Bake 35 minutes in a 400 degree oven.

The Inn at Duck Creek
Sitting in the heart of Wellfleet's historic village, this is Cape Cod at its best.

Wellfleet, Massachusetts
70 Main St., Box 364 ~ Wellfleet, MA 02667 ~ 508-349-9333

The Inn at Starlight Lake

Chocolate Walnut Pie

1	pound butter
4	unsweetened chocolates
4	cups sugar
8	eggs
8	teaspoons evaporated milk
1	teaspoon vanilla

Melt butter and chocolates together. Mix with sugar, eggs, evaporated milk and vanilla. Line two 10-inch pie crusts with walnuts and pour mix into it. Bake at 375 degrees for 55-60 minutes.

The Inn at Starlight Lake
This old fashioned inn has welcomed visitors to the Appalachian Mountains since 1902.

Starlight, Pennsylvania
Rt. 370 ~ P.O. Box 27 ~ Starlight, PA 18461 ~ 570-798-2519

Widow McCrae House

Baked Pears with Honey

4	fresh ripe pears (Anjou, Bosc or Comice)
2	tablespoons butter or marjarine
4	tablespoons honey
4	tablespoons grated lemon rind
4	tablespoons fresh lemon juice
2	tablespoons water
2	tablespoons chopped almonds or walnuts
	Whipped cream or vanilla ice cream (optional)
	Mint sprigs

Rinse, halve and core unpeeled pears. Place them cut side up in a well-buttered baking dish. Fill pear halves with the butter and honey. Sprinkle with lemon rind. Combine the lemon juice and water. Pour over pear halves. Bake at 350 degrees for about 20 minutes, or until pears are tender. Top with chopped almonds or walnuts. Serve pears, still warm, with whipped cream or vanilla ice cream, if desired. Garnish with fresh mint sprigs.

Widow McCrae House

A Beautiful Victorian Bed & Breakfast, located a two-minute walk from Frenchtown's charming shops, restaurants and the Delaware River.

Frenchtown, New Jersey
53 Kingwood Ave. ~ Frenchtown, NJ 08825 ~ 908-996-4999

Longfellow's
Wayside Inn

Rhubarb Pie

5   cups diced rhubarb stalk
1   tablespoon cornstarch
5   fresh strawberries
1½ cups sugar
     pastry crust for 9-inch pie

Mix all ingredients in bowl and place in unbaked pie crust. Egg wash rim and place top crust over filling. Crimp edges and cut steam vents in crust. Egg wash and bake in 350 degree oven until golden brown.

Longfellow's Wayside Inn
This is where early Americans conspired revolution against the British that led to the birth of our country.

Sudbury, Massachusetts
72 Wayside Inn Rd. ~ Sudbury, MA 01776-3206 ~ 978-443-1776

The Lyme Inn

Brandy Alexander Pie

Crust: 6 tablespoons melted butter
1½ cups finely crushed chocolate wafer crumbs

Mix melted butter and wafer crumbs well before patting firmly into 9-inch pan, covering bottom and sides. Either chill thoroughly before filling or bake at 350 degrees for 15 minutes.

Filling: 1 envelope unflavored gelatin
⅔ cup sugar
2 eggs, separated
2 cups heavy cream, whipped
1 9-inch chocolate crumb crust
½ cup cold water
⅛ teaspoon salt
¼ cup cognac
¼ cup crème de cacao

Sprinkle gelatin over cold water in saucepan. Add ⅓ cup of sugar, salt, and egg yolks, stirring to blend. Heat over low while stirring until gelatin dissolves and mixture thickens. Remove from heat and stir in cognac and crème de cacao. Chill until mixture starts to mound slightly. Beat egg whites until stiff. Gradually beat in remaining sugar and fold into gelatin mixture. Fold in 1 cup whipped cream. Turn into crust. Chill. Top with whipped cream.

The Lyme Inn

There are ten fireplaces and four floors filled with antiques and comfort, dating back to 1809.

Lyme, New Hampshire Lyme, NH 03768 ~ 603-795-2222 or 4404

Northeast Region

The Mainstay Inn

Lemon Pound Cake

1½ cups butter
3⅓ cups sugar
5   eggs
2   teaspoons vanilla
3⅓ cups cake flour
½   teaspoon baking powder
1   tablespoon grated lemon rind
1   cup buttermilk
¼   cup lemon juice

Grease and flour 10-inch tube pan. Combine butter and 3 cups sugar and beat until fluffy. Add eggs, one at a time. Add vanilla. In another bowl, combine the flour, baking powder, and lemon rind. Add flour to butter mixture alternately with buttermilk. Pour into prepared pan and bake at 300 degrees for 2 hours.

Meanwhile, combine lemon juice with ⅓ cup sugar and cook about 2 minutes. When cake is done, remove from pan and brush with lemon glaze.

Blueberry Peach Pie

Prepare a 2-quart ovenproof baking dish with oil spray. Preheat oven to 350 degrees.

Filling:
- 1½ cups sour cream
- 1 large egg
- 1 cup sugar
- ¼ cup flour
- 1 teaspoon vanilla extract
- 1 pint fresh blueberries
- 5 large ripe peaches (peeled and sliced)

Beat sour cream, egg, sugar, flour and vanilla. Add blueberries and peaches and bake 20 minutes.

Topping:
- 1 stick butter
- ½ cup flour
- ⅓ cup brown sugar
- 1 tablespoon cinnamon
- 1 cup chopped pecans

Combine butter, flour, brown sugar, cinnamon and nuts. Sprinkle over hot filling. Return to oven and bake 15 minutes. Serve warm. Makes 8-10 servings.

Hummingbird Cake

3 cups flour
1½ teaspoons vanilla
2 cups sugar
1 teaspoon salt
1½ cups cooking oil
1 8-ounce can crushed pineapple, undrained
1 teaspoon soda
1 teaspoon cinnamon
3 eggs
2 cups diced bananas
1 cup chopped pecans

Preheat oven to 325 degrees. Grease tube pan. Sift dry ingredients and add pineapple, oil, vanilla, eggs, bananas, and pecans, mixing by hand until just blended. Bake 1 hour. Serves 10-12.

The Mainstay Inn
Built as an exclusive men's club in 1872, and its well-appointed guest rooms are reminders of those opulent days.

Cape May, New Jersey
635 Columbia Ave. ~ Cape May, NJ 08204-2305 ~ 609-884-8690

Mohonk Mountain House

Mohonk Cabinet Pudding

3   cups stale Danish, cut into 14-inch cubes
2   tablespoons raisins
3   eggs
5   tablespoons sugar
    pinch salt
2   cups milk
1   teaspoon vanilla

In a 1 ½-quart glass baking dish, place stale Danish cubes. Add raisins. To prepare custard, beat eggs, sugar and salt with wire whisk. Gradually beat in milk and vanilla. Pour custard over Danish-raisin mixture and sprinkle with cinnamon. Set baking dish in larger pan and fill with water to halfway up sides of baking dish. Bake at 375 degrees until knife inserted comes out clean, approximately 1 hour. Serve warm at room temperature. Serves 4-6.

Mohonk Mountain House

With seven stories of polished woodwork, this inn is one-eighth of a mile long.

New Paltz, New York

1000 Mountain Rest Rd. ~ Lake Mohonk, New Paltz, NY 12561 ~ 845-255-1000

Old Drovers Inn

Old Drovers Inn Key Lime Pie

5   egg yolks
19   ounces sweetened condensed milk
4   ounces freshly squeezed lime juice
      grated rind from one lime
1   8-inch graham cracker crust

Beat egg yolk with wire whisk, and blend in condensed milk, add lime juice and grated lime. Pour into crust and refrigerate for two hours.

Old Drovers Inn
This inn continues to offer fine food and lodging to travelers just as it did when it catered to the cattle drovers in 1750.

Dover Plains, New York
196 East Duncan Hill Blvd. ~ Dover Plains, NY 12522-5604 ~ 845-832-9311

Old Fort Inn

Strawberry Delight

1	10-ounce package butter cookies
¾	cup butter
1	cup powdered sugar
2	eggs
⅓	cup chopped walnuts
1	quart strawberries (cut in half)
½	pint whipping cream

Roll cookies into crumbs. Cover bottom of 8-inch square pan with half of the crumbs. Thoroughly cream butter and sugar. Add eggs 1 at a time and beat very very well. Spread mix over crumbs. Sprinkle with walnuts and top with berries. Spread with whipped cream and sprinkle with remaining crumbs. Garnish with whole berries. Chill thoroughly.

Old Fort Inn
Returning visitors come year after year to this secluded seaside resort.

Kennebunkport, Maine
Eight Old Fort Ave. ~ PO Box M ~ Kennebunkport, ME 04046 ~ 800-828-3678

Frozen Lemon Pie

1	graham cracker crust
	juice and rind of 1 lemon
3	egg whites, stiff
1	cup cream
3	egg yolks well beaten
½	cup sugar
1	teaspoon sugar

To egg yolks add ½ cup sugar along with juice and rind of lemon. Beat 3 egg whites stiff with 1 teaspoon sugar and fold into egg yolk mixture. Beat 1 cup cream stiff and fold into all ingredients. Place in graham cracker crust and freeze. Makes one delicious 9-inch pie.

Philbrook Farm Inn
With spectacular scenery, this inn is perfect for artists and writers. Listed on the national register.

Shelburne, New Hampshire
881 North Rd. ~ Shelburne, NH 03581-3212~ 603-466-3831

THE QUEEN ANNE
inn & resort
CHATHAM · CAPE COD

Queen Anne Inn Apple Pie

Crust:
2¾ cups flour
1 cup butter
1 cup and 3 tablespoons confectioner's sugar
1 pinch salt
1 drop vanilla extract
½ teaspoon finely chopped lemon zest
½ teaspoon finely chopped orange zest

Sift flour into a bowl. Make a depression in the center. Dice the butter and place it in the center. Mix flour and butter into a fine, well blended mixture using finger tips. Add all other seasonings. Knead the mixture into a medium firm dough. Let the dough rest for a minimum of one hour. Preheat oven to 380 degrees. Set ⅓ of dough aside for top of pie. Roll dough into flat square (⅛-inch thickness). Place the dough in a 9-inch metal pie pan which has been greased and lightly sprayed with flour.

⅓ cup sliced almonds
¼ cup bread crumbs

Mix together almonds and bread crumbs and place in pie pan over bottom of pie dough.

Continued on page 62

Northeast Region

Continued from page 61

Filling:	5	large McIntosh apples, peeled and sliced into ¼-inch pieces
	1	teaspoon cinnamon
	¼	cup granulated sugar (to taste)
	2	tablespoons lemon juice
	1	tablespoon rum
	1	drop vanilla extract

Mix ingredients well and let sit for 30 minutes. Place filling in pie shell, over almond and bread crumb layer. Cover with remaining dough. Trim and decorate crust and rim.
Brush crust evenly with egg wash (1 egg yolk lightly beaten). Bake at 380 degrees for 40 minutes. Serve fresh and warm with whipped cream.

The Queen Anne Inn
Visitors to this charming inn enjoy old Cape Cod at its best.

Cape Cod, Massachusetts
70 Queen Anne Rd. ~ Chatham, Cape Cod, MA, 02633 ~ 800-545-4667

Caramel Apple Tarts

Crust: | 1 | cup flour
½ | teaspoon salt
½ | teaspoon sugar
3 | tablespoons cold butter
3 | tablespoons vegetable shortening
3 | tablespoons ice water

Combine flour, salt and sugar. Cut in butter and shortening. Toss with enough ice water to bind. Divide dough into quarters and flatten into small discs. Wrap and refrigerate at least one hour.

Filling: | ½ | cup sugar
4 | apples, peeled, cored and sliced
1 | teaspoon cinnamon
½ | teaspoon nutmeg
water
pinch of cream of tartar

Heat sugar and water and cream of tartar in sauté pan, swirling in pan until it caramelizes. Add apples and sauté until tender. Season with cinnamon and nutmeg. Remove dough from refrigerator. Roll into a circle and divide filling evenly between four circles, leaving one inch around edge free. Crimp edges by folding dough back over itself. Bake at 350 degrees until golden brown, approximately 15-20 minutes. Serve with ice cream, whipped cream or crème fraîche.
May be made with peaches, pears or any sautéed fruit.

Northeast Region

Chocolate Macadamia Nut Tart

Crusts: 1½ cups flour
              ¾   cup confectioner's sugar
              ½   cup cocoa powder
              1   cup butter
              1   teaspoon vanilla
                   pinch of salt

Put all ingredients in a Cuisinart. Blend until it forms a ball. Cut in half, and form into two discs. Freeze one for future use.

Between two pieces of waxed paper, roll out one of the discs into a 10-inch circle. Take one half of wax paper off and slip it into a 9-inch tart pan. Remove other piece of wax paper. Bake at 350 degrees for 15 minutes. Let cool.

Filling: 1½ cups toasted Macadamias or hazelnuts
              8   ounces high quality bittersweet chocolate, chopped
              1   cup heavy cream

Pour nuts into tart shell. Place chocolate in a bowl. Bring cream to a boil, then pour over chocolate. Let sit for one minute. Whisk until smooth. Pour over the nuts in the tart pan. Refrigerate.

Black and White Chocolate Macaroon Tart

Shell: 3   cups coconut
                  1/3 cup sugar
                  2   egg whites
                  2   tablespoons flour

Line bottom of tart pan with parchment paper or wax paper. Combine all of the above ingredients. Put into pan. Bake at 375 degrees for 20 minutes.

Filling: 6   ounces white chocolate
              6   ounces dark chocolate
            2/3 cup sour cream
              2   egg yolks
            2/3 cup heavy cream
              2   tablespoons rum

Melt white chocolate in a double boiler. Combine with sour cream, then set aside. Over double boiler, heat and stir egg yolks and heavy cream until thick. Add dark chocolate, and heat until melted. Remove from heat and add rum. Spoon into tart shell, alternating one dollop white, one dollop dark. When all in swirl with a knife until marbled. Chill.

Northeast Region

Chocolate Apricot Cheesecake

20 ounces cream cheese, room temperature
½ cup sour cream
½ cup confectioner's sugar
6 ounces white chocolate, melted
3 eggs
½ cup apricot preserves, warmed
  juice of one lemon

Blend cream cheese and sour cream until smooth. Add sugar, lemon juice and white chocolate. Mix until blended. Add eggs, one at a time, beating just until incorporated. Do not overbeat. Pour into 8-inch crust. Drizzle apricot preserves on top. Swirl in with a knife. Bake at 325 degrees for about 1¼ hours or until let. Turn oven off, and let sit in oven for an hour. Remove and chill thoroughly.

Red Clover Inn
Twelve delightful guest rooms are surrounded by the natural beauty of Vermont.

Mendon, Vermont
7 Woodward Rd. ~ Mendon, VT 05701 ~ 800-752-0571

THE RED LION INN

Indian Pudding

4	cups milk
4	tablespoons butter
½	cup cornmeal
½	cup molasses
¼	cup sugar
1	cup chopped apples
½	cup raisins
4½	teaspoons cinnamon
1½	teaspoons ginger
½	teaspoon salt
1	egg

Combine 2½ cups milk with butter and scald. Combine ½ cup milk and cornmeal, add to scalded milk and butter. Cook 20 minutes, stirring slowly so mixture does not burn. Add molasses, sugar, apples and raisins. Stir in cinnamon, ginger, salt and egg. Cook 5 more minutes. Pour into well-greased shallow pan. Pour remaining cup of milk over this, and bake at 325 degrees for 1½ hours or until pudding is set. Serve warm with ice cream or whipped cream. Serves 8-10.

The Red Lion Inn

This inn appeared in one of Norman Rockwell's Christmas scenes and has hosted five U.S. Presidents as well as Nathaniel Hawthorne, William Cullen Bryant and Henry Wadsworth Longfellow.

Stockbridge, Massachusetts

30 Main St. ~ Stockbridge, MA 01262 ~ 413-298-5545

Northeast Region

Richardson's Canal House

Raspberry Frangipane Tart

Dough:	1	pound butter
	¾	pound sugar
	½	pound cake flour
	½	pound bread flour
	½	teaspoon baking powder
	½	teaspoon salt
	½	teaspoon lemon extract
	½	teaspoon orange extract
	3	eggs

Cream butter and sugar together. Add dry ingredients, mix well. Add eggs, one at a time. Stir in extracts. Form dough into a ball, wrap in plastic and chill 2 hours.

Spray a tart pan with pan release spray. Press dough into pan with fingers, dock dough and bake 10-12 minutes at 350 degrees. Cool in pan. Makes 12-15 small tarts or 1 12-inch tart.

Batter:	8	ounces almond paste

1¾	sticks unsalted butter
1	cup sugar
5	large eggs
1	teaspoon vanilla extract
1	teaspoon almond extract
2¼	cups all-purpose flour

Combine almond paste, butter and sugar. Blend well. Add eggs, one at a time, mixing well after each addition. Add extracts. Mix in flour, only enough to incorporate. Spoon batter into tart pan and smooth top. Bake 10 minutes at 350 degrees. Cool.

Richardson's Canal House
This registered landmark has been elegantly restored to reflect its New England farmhouse look.

Pittsford, New York
1474 Marsh Road ~ Pittsford, NY 14534 ~ 585-248-5000

Rockhouse Mountain Farm

Pumpkin Chiffon Pie

3   eggs, separated
½   cup sugar
1¼ cups canned pumpkin
⅔   cup milk
½   teaspoon salt
½   teaspoon cinnamon
½   teaspoon ginger
1   tablespoon gelatin
¼   cup cold water

In a double boiler, cook egg yolks, ½ cup sugar, pumpkin, milk, salt, cinnamon and ginger until thick. Soften gelatin in cold water, then add to mixture and cool. Beat egg whites until stiff, then gently fold into mixture. Add sugar gradually, and garnish with whipped cream.

Rockhouse Almond Cake

1   cup sifted flour
¾   cup sugar
½   cup buttermilk
⅓   cup margarine, melted and cooled
½   tablespoon baking powder
½   teaspoon soda
½   teaspoon vanilla
½   teaspoon almond extract
¼   teaspoon salt
     sliced almonds

Sift dry ingredients together. Beat wet ingredients well, and add to the sifted dry ingredients. Stir just until liquid is absorbed. Bake in a spring form pan at 350 degrees for about 30 minutes. While hot, cover with sliced almonds and add hot syrup.

Syrup: ¾   cup sugar
           6   tablespoons water
           ½   teaspoon almond extract

Boil ingredients to 220 degrees, and pour over the cake and almonds. Then broil 6 to 8 inches from the heat until almonds are golden.

Northeast Region

Log Roll

4	eggs
¾	cup sugar
¼	cup sifted flour
¼	cup dry cocoa
¼	teaspoon baking powder
¼	teaspoon salt

Grease a cookie sheet, line with wax paper, then grease again.
Combine eggs and sugar and beat the dickens out of them. Sift the remaining ingredients and fold gently into the egg mixture with a whisk. Pour into the cookie sheet and bake at 300 degrees for about 25 minutes. Watch carefully so that the edges do not get hard. Turn upside down on a towel sprinkled with granulated sugar. Fold up as a jelly roll.

Filling:	2	cups heavy cream
	¼	cup confectioner's sugar
	4	teaspoons instant coffee
	1	teaspoon vanilla

Whip ingredients together. Use half of the cream for filling, and the other half for topping. Decorate with chocolate curls.

Chiffon Cake

2¼ cups sifted cake flour
1¼ cups sugar
¾ cup cold water
½ cup salad oil
5 eggs, separated
3 teaspoons baking powder
2 teaspoons vanilla, lemon, orange or almond flavoring
1 teaspoon salt
½ teaspoon cream of tartar

Sift together flour, sugar, baking powder and salt. Mix together egg yolks, water, oil and flavoring, and combine them with the dry. Beat for one minute with electric mixer. Combine egg whites with cream of tartar and beat until stiff. Combine batter and whites gently. Bake in tube pan at 325 degrees for about 45 minutes. Invert to cool.

Rockhouse Mountain Farm
This inn has provided good food and lodging since 1946.

Eaton Center, New Hampshire
PO Box 90 ~ Eaton Center, NH 03832-0090 ~ 603-447-2880

The Sherwood Inn

Burnt Creme

12 egg yolks
1 tablespoon vanilla extract
½ pint heavy cream
21 ounces sweetened condensed milk

Over medium heat scald milk and heavy cream. Temper the yolks with the hot mixture, then add yolks. Remove from heat, add vanilla and pour into ramekins, being certain to fill to rim. Bake in water bath at 350 degrees for 20-25 minutes or until just browned. Cool. Cover custards with 1 tablespoon granulated sugar, then caramelize sugar with the broiler or an iron. Brown sugar can be substituted. Serves 12-14.

The Sherwood Inn
This old stage coach tavern was a favorite stop for the Knickerbocker Tours in the 1820s.

Skaneateles, New York
26 West Genesee St. ~ Skaneateles, NY 13152 ~ 315-685-3405

Shire Inn

Shire Inn

Baked Pear

2   Anjou pears
1   cup sugar
4   tablespoons vanilla extract
     sliced almonds
1   teaspoon almond extract
1   cup heavy cream
     semi-sweet chocolate, melted

Preheat oven to 350 degrees. Halve pears, core and peel. In four ramekin cups, sprinkle ½ cup sugar in each. Place pear half on top of sugar and pour 1 tablespoon of vanilla extract and ¼ teaspoon almond extract over each pear. Make for 25-30 minutes.

Pour ¼ cup cream over each pear and continue baking for 20-30 more minutes. Remove from oven and cool for 5 minutes before serving.

If ramekins are not available, use casserole dish. Garnish with sliced almonds and pour chocolate over each pear. Serves 4.

75   *Northeast Region*

Praline Custard Pie

Filling:
	4	eggs
	1	cup milk
	2	cups heavy cream
	½	biscuit mix
	¼	pound butter
	1	cup sugar
	1	teaspoon nutmeg
	1	teaspoon cinnamon
	1	teaspoon vanilla extract

Blend all ingredients in blender at high speed. Pour into greased 9-inch pie plate. Bake at 350 degrees for 45 minutes.

Topping:
	⅓	cup packed brown sugar
	⅓	cup chopped pecans
	1	tablespoon softened butter

Mix ingredients together, spread onto custard. Cook for 10 minutes. May be served with warm caramel topping. Serves 8.

Shire Inn

This inn traces its beginning back to 1832. At this registered landmark, five course dinners await the visitor.

277 VT Route 110 ~ Chelsea, VT 05038 ~ 802-685-3031

Snowville Inn

Decadent Chocolate Cake

1   pound good quality bittersweet chocolate
½   cup plus 2 tablespoons unsalted butter
4   eggs, room temperature
1   tablespoon sugar
1   tablespoon flour

Melt the chocolate and butter together in a bowl over a water bath. Set aside to cool slightly.

In another bowl over simmering water, whip eggs and sugar with a hand mixer until tripled in volume (be patient!), fold in flour. Fold in chocolate mixture very gently. Pour into well greased and paper lined 9-inch springform pan. Bake at 425 degrees for 12-15 minutes. Do not overcook. Cool and set aside. Top with:

6   ounces semisweet chocolate
2   ounces vegetable shortening

Melt together and place in a well-greased plastic lined bread pan. Cool until set then allow to come to room temperature. Peel with a vegetable peeler to get large curls. Decorate top of cake with curls and dust lightly with powdered sugar.

Snowville Inn
Genuine hospitality and personal service define this inn.

Snowville, New Hampshire
246 Stewart Rd. ~ Snowville, NH 03832 ~ 603-447-2818

Chocolate Sauce

2 tablespoons butter
1 cup milk
⅔ cup sugar
1½ squares unsweetened chocolate

Combine all ingredients in a double boiler and cook over medium heat. Dribble over rich ice cream. Makes 4 Servings.

Springside Inn
Established in 1851 as a boys' school, it probably served as a station on the Underground Railroad.

Auburn, New York
6141 West Lake Rd. ~ Auburn, NY 13021 ~ 315-252-7247

THE 🦋 WAUWINET

Molten Chocolate Cake

14 ounces chocolate
14 ounces butter
8   egg yolks
8   eggs
9   ounces confectionery sugar

Melt butter and chocolate. In a separate bowl, whisk egg yolks and eggs. Add chocolate. Add sugar to this mix. Let sit for one half hour. Add mix to single serving Teflon molds or single serving molds from which the bottoms pop out.

Bake at 400 degrees for five minutes. Remove from oven and invert onto plate. Serve with your favorite ice cream. Dust plate and cake with powdered sugar.

The Wauwinet
Lends itself beautifully to the natural wonders of Nantucket. Twenty guest rooms and a cluster of delightful cottages await your pleasure.

Nantucket, Massachusetts
P.O. Box 2580 ~ Nantucket, MA 02584 ~ 800-426-8718 ~ 508-228-0145

Pecan Cream Cheese Pie

1	9-inch pastry shell partially baked, or graham cracker shell
16	ounces cream cheese
½	cup finely chopped, toasted pecans
¼	cup sugar
4	eggs
¾	cup light corn syrup
3	teaspoons vanilla

Preheat oven to 375 degrees. Combine cream cheese, sugar, 1 egg 2 teaspoons of vanilla. Beat until smooth. Spread evenly into shell; sprinkle with pecans.

Into separate bowl, beat 3 eggs, 1 teaspoon vanilla, corn syrup and 2 tablespoons sugar until blended. Pour lightly over pecans. Bake until set completely, about 45-60 minutes. Chill. Serves 8.

Cinnamon Swirl Cobbler

Filling:
6 cups mixed fruit (blueberries, blackberries, cherries, apples, etc.)
3 tablespoons flour
1 cup sugar
1 teaspoon cinnamon
¼ teaspoon nutmeg
4 tablespoons butter or margarine

Mix all ingredients and heat in pan on stove to a boil. Stir well and pour into greased 13 x 9-inch pan.

Topping:
2⅔ cups Bisquick
¼ cup sugar
4 tablespoons sugar
4 tablespoons melted butter
2 tablespoons softened butter
⅔ cup milk
1 teaspoon cinnamon

Mix Bisquick with 4 tablespoons sugar, melted butter and milk until soft dough forms; beat 20 strokes. Smooth dough into ball on well-floured board. Knead 8-10 times. Split dough in half. Roll each half into 9-inch squares, spread with softened butter and ¼ cup sugar mixed with cinnamon. Roll up, seal well and slice in ¾-inch slices. Place dough from both halves, cut sides up, on hot berries. Bake at 350 degrees 30-45 minutes until dough is lightly browned and cooked through. Serve warm with ice cream.

Cherry Crumble Squares

3 cups flour
3 teaspoons baking powder
1 teaspoon salt
1 cup sugar
1 cup vegetable shortening
1 can cherry pie filling
2 beaten eggs
1 teaspoon vanilla
½ teaspoon almond flavoring

Mix together flour, baking powder and salt; add sugar, then cut in vegetable shortening. Add eggs, vanilla and almond flavoring. Mix and toss with fork. Pat ¾ batter into 13 x 9-inch, ungreased pan. Add pie filling, then sprinkle with remaining batter and bake at 350 degrees for about 45 minutes, until lightly browned.

The Wedgewood Inn
This beautiful Victorian inn with its inviting wrap-around porch has welcomed visitors since 1950.

New Hope, Pennsylvania
111 West Bridge St. ~ New Hope, PA 18938 ~ 215-862-2570

West Mountain Inn

Chocolate Sour Cream Cake

1   cup water
2   cups flour
2   cups sugar
2   eggs
⅔   cup sour cream
¼   cup vegetable oil
1   teaspoon baking soda
½   teaspoon baking powder
3   ounces unsweetened baker's chocolate
1   teaspoon vanilla

Combine all ingredients in a bowl, mixing well. Bake in 350 degree oven for about 45 minutes or until toothpick comes out clean. Frost with a mocha frosting.

French Silk Pie

Crust: 5   ounces Nabisco chocolate wafers (crushed)
             4   tablespoons melted butter

Combine and press into pie plate to form crust.

Filling: 6   ounces semisweet chocolate melted and cooled to
                room temperature
          ½   cup butter softened
          1   cup sugar
          4   eggs

Cream butter and sugar. Add cooled chocolate and mix until blended. Add 2 eggs, and whip for 5 minutes. Add remaining two eggs and whip 5 minutes longer. Pour into chocolate wafer crust and freeze for 1½ hours. Top with whipped cream and chocolate shavings.

West Mountain Inn

West Mountain Inn is home to professionals from the arts and crafts as well as other visitors who find the inn an ideal place to be.

Arlington, Vermont

144 West Mountain Inn Rd. ~ Arlington, VT 05250 ~ 802-375-6516

Southeast Region

Southeast Region

Sweet Memories

The Baliwick Inn

Melting Chocolate Cake with Coffee Ice Cream

6 ounces bittersweet chocolate
3½ ounces butter, room temperature
2 eggs, room temperature
2 egg yolks, room temperature
3½ ounces sugar
1½ ounces flour, sifted
cocoa powder

Melt chocolate and butter in a double boiler. Whip eggs, yolks and sugar to the ribbon (pale yellow). Sift flour into eggs and fold. Then fold mixture into chocolate. Do not overwork!!

Butter cake rings and parchment paper and dust with cocoa powder, and fill ¾ full with batter. Bake at 350 degrees for about 10 minutes. Let cool for a minute, then unmold. Serve warm with coffee ice cream. Can garnish with Russian butter cookies.

The Baliwick Inn
This charming inn is located in the heart of the city.

Fairfax, Virginia
4023 Chain Bridge Rd. ~ Fairfax, VA 22030 ~ 703-691-2266

Coconut Banana Crème Brulee

Custard: 1   cup sweetened cream of coconut
1½ cups heavy cream
5   egg yolks
3   whole eggs
⅓   cup sugar
½   teaspoon salt
½   teaspoon ground nutmeg
1   tablespoon vanilla extract
1   tablespoon dark rum
½   cup shredded coconut
Brulee: 2   bananas, sliced thin
6   teaspoons sugar

In a saucepan heat cream, cream of coconut, salt and nutmeg until just simmering. Remove from heat. In a bowl mix together remaining ingredients with a fork until smooth, do not incorporate a lot of air. Slowly add in hot cream mixture stirring to incorporate. Butter soufflé dishes and fill with custard. Bake in a water bath in 300 degree oven 25-30 minutes. A knife inserted in the center should come out clean. Cool till ready to serve. Run a thin knife around the edge of soufflé dish and remove custard from dish, arrange sliced bananas on top and sprinkle each with 1 teaspoon of sugar. Brown with a propane torch or use a broiler.

The Beaufort Inn
Built in the late 1800's and painted Charleston salmon. Afternoon tea.

Beaufort, South Carolina
809 Port Republic St. ~ Beaufort, SC 29902 ~ 843-521-9000

Beaumont Inn

Chess Pie

1	cup white sugar
1	level tablespoon flour
¼	teaspoon salt
¼	pound (½ cup) melted butter
2	egg yolks
¼	cup water
1	whole egg
1	teaspoon white vinegar

Mix flour, sugar and salt together. Beat the egg yolks and the one whole egg together adding water, vinegar and melted butter. Beat well, then add flour, sugar and salt mixture. Pour into an unbaked pie shell and bake at 350 degrees until set, about 35 minutes.

Topping: 2 egg whites
          1 tablespoon white sugar

Mix ingredients together and beat until stiff. Spread on top of pie and brown at 250 degrees for 12 minutes.

Beaumont Inn

Listed on the national register, this graceful old inn with its gilded mirrors, velvets and swags, has been operated by the Dedmans for four generations.

Harrodsburg, Kentucky

638 Beaumont Inn Dr. ~ P.O. Box 158 ~ Harrodsburg, KY 40330-0158 ~ 859-734-3381

Southeast Region

The BOAR'S HEAD INN

Southern Pecan Pie

3   eggs, slightly beaten
¾   cup dark corn syrup
¾   cup light corn syrup
2   tablespoons melted butter
⅛   teaspoon salt
1   teaspoon vanilla
1   tablespoon flour
1   cup pecans
1   teaspoon sugar
1   unbaked 9-inch pastry shell

Mix flour, sugar, salt, and butter until creamy and blend in light and dark syrups, eggs, and vanilla. Spread pecans over bottom of pie shell and pour in the mixture. Bake at 325 degrees for 1 hour or until firm.

The Boar's Head Inn
This luxury estate with its wide range of sports facilities is located in the foothills of the Blue Ridge Mountains.

Charlottesville, Virginia
200 Ednam Dr. ~ Charlottesville, VA 22903 (just west of Charlottesville off Rte. 250) ~ 434-296-2181

Boone Tavern Hotel

German Lemon Roll

6   eggs
1   cup sugar
1   cup cake flour
1   tablespoon lemon juice
¾   tablespoon grated lemon rind
½   teaspoon vanilla
¼   teaspoon salt

Beat egg whites until stiff, and add half of the sugar by folding in with long strokes incorporating as much air into the mixture as possible. Beat the yolks until lemon colored, add remaining sugar, lemon rind, juice, salt and vanilla. Beat well. Fold this into the egg whites using long, careful stroke incorporating as much air as possible into the mixture. Fold in the flour by the same method. Place in a 12 x 18-inch cookie pan, ungreased. Bake for 25 minutes at 325 degrees. Allow to cool for 10 minutes. Turn out onto a piece of wax paper and place a sheet of wax paper over the top. Now roll up as for a jelly roll and twist the ends of the paper to secure the roll together. Allow to cool.

Continued on page 92

Continued from page 91

Filling: 2   **cups whipped cream**
4   **tablespoons lemon juice**
2   **tablespoons grated lemon rind**

Fold the lemon juice and rind into the whipped cream.
Unroll the cake, remove the wax paper and spread the filling over the roll.
Again roll the cake up as tightly as possible without breaking it and wrap in wax paper. Place in refrigerator for 1 hour or longer.
Slice and serve with a dash of sweetened whipped cream.

Boone Tavern Hotel
This stately hotel with its pillars and porches has played a rich part in the economic and cultural life of Berea since 1909. Three gracious meals are served daily by a student staff of smiling faces.

Berea, Kentucky
100 Main St. ~ Berea, KY 40403 ~ 859-985-3700

BUTTONWOOD INN

Fluffy Banana Cake

2¼ cups cake flour, unsifted
½ teaspoon salt
⅔ cups shortening
3 eggs
1⅔ cups sugar
1¼ teaspoon each baking powder and soda
¾ cup mashed banana
1¼ cup milk

Preheat oven to 350 degrees. Cream shortening and sugar, add eggs. Mix well. At medium speed gradually add banana. Mix. At low speed add flour mixture alternately with milk, ending with flour. Pour into 2 floured and greased 8-inch cake pans. Bake 30-40 minutes. Cool. Top with:

Banana Icing:
One (15.4 ounce) package vanilla white frosting mix (use package directions), mixed with ¼ cup mashed banana.
Optional: Over hot water melt 1 square (1 ounce) semi-sweet chocolate and ¼ teaspoon shortening. Drizzle over cake.

Southeast Region

John's Buttermilk Pie

3 eggs, separate (whites should be room temperature)
4 tablespoons margarine, melted and cooled.
2 cups buttermilk
1 cup sugar
3 tablespoons flour
½ teaspoon salt
2 unbaked, unpricked 9-inch pie shells

Preheat oven to 375 degrees. Beat egg yolks, add margarine and buttermilk. Combine sugar, flour and salt. Mix in egg mixture. Beat egg whites and fold into mix. Pour into pie shells and bake for 35-45 minutes. Pie is done when toothpick comes out clean. Cool. Can be served room temperature; refrigerate leftovers, serve cold.

Chocolate Amaretto Pie

Filling:
3	cups miniature marshmallows
½	cup milk
1	cup whipping cream
¼	cup amaretto
2	ounces semisweet chocolate, melted and cooled

Heat marshmallows and milk until melted. Refrigerate 25 minutes, until thick. Add amaretto and chocolate. Beat whipping cream until stiff peaks form. Fold into marshmallow mixture. Pour into 9-inch cookie crust. Recipe follows:

Crust:

Combine 1½ cups chocolate wafer cookies with ¼ cup margarine and mix well. Pour into buttered 9-inch pie plate.
Refrigerate pie several hours before serving. Top with amaretto whipping cream.

Topping:

Whip 1 cup whipping cream until stiff. Beat in 2 tablespoons powdered sugar and 2 tablespoons amaretto. Chill.

Buttonwood Inn

Nestled among tall pines, this inn is a delight for people who enjoy simplicity and the rustic beauty of Mother Nature.

Franklin, North Carolina

50 Admiral Dr. ~ Franklin, NC 28734-1981 ~ 828-369-8985

Canaan Land Farm

Pound Cake

3	sticks butter
3	cups sugar
3	cups flour
1	cup milk
6	eggs
1	teaspoon lemon extract

Cream sugar and butter, add eggs and beat well. Add milk and flour alternately, beating each time. Add lemon extract. Bake 325 degrees in a greased and floured tube pan for 1½ hours.

Icing:	1	box confectioner's sugar
	8	tablespoons Crisco
	8	tablespoons butter
	6	tablespoons milk
	1	teaspoon lemon

Cream butter and Crisco, add sugar and milk. Beat, then add lemon.

Canaan Land Farm
Filled with antiques, this registered landmark is secluded in the bluegrass region of Kentucky.

Harrodsburg, Kentucky
700 Canaan Land Rd. ~ Harrodsburg, KY 40330 ~ 859-734-3984

Butterscotch Toffee Cake

1½ cups whipping cream, whipped
5½ ounces butterscotch syrup (topping)
½ teaspoon vanilla (preferred pure from Mexico)
1 angel food cake
¾ pound English toffee (or Almond Rocca), crushed

Whip cream until it starts to thicken. Add syrup and vanilla slowly and continue beating until thick. Cut cake into 3 layers, spread whipped cream on layers and sprinkle with toffee. Put layers together. Frost top and sides with whipped cream and sprinkle with remaining toffee. Refrigerate at least 6 hours.
Note: Put Almond Rocca through meat grinder to crush easily.

Lemon Apricot Cake

1 lemon cake mix
1 17-ounce can apricot halves
(unpeeled, undrained, no pits)
3 eggs
1 10-ounce jar apricot jam

Combine mix, apricots and syrup, and eggs in large bowl. Bake in very well greased bundt or tube pan for 40-45 minutes at 350 degrees. Cool for 15 minutes before removing. When cold, heat jam and pour over cake and cool. Even if the pan is teflon, grease well and lightly flour.

Quick Cherry Dessert Cake

1   teaspoon lemon juice
2   cans cherry pie filling
2   packages Duncan Hines white cake mix
2   sticks melted butter
1   cup pecans
1   pint whipping cream

Add lemon juice to pie filling. Spread pie filling on bottom of lightly greased or sprayed 13 x 9 x 2-inch pan. Combine dry cake mix and melted butter and nuts. Sprinkle over pie filling. Bake at 350 degrees for 40-50 minutes until lightly browned. Top with whipped cream.

Sherried Nuts

1   cup sugar
½   cup cream sherry
1   teaspoon cinnamon
1   teaspoon vanilla
2   cups nuts (walnuts or pecans)
    pinch of cream of tartar

Combine sugar, cream sherry and cream of tartar in saucepan and cook to 234 degrees. Remove from heat and add cinnamon and vanilla. Stir in nuts and stir until cool.

Cedar Ridge by Request
Surrounded by the natural beauty of native trees and colorful wild flowers, this rustic but elegant resort is the perfect romantic getaway in all seasons.
Mount Vernon, Kentucky
Route 6, Lake Linville Road ~ Mt. Vernon, KY 40456 ~ 606-256-0037

Cedar Rock Farm Bed & Breakfast

Grammy's Chess Pie

1   stick margarine
1½ cups sugar
3   eggs
1   teaspoon vinegar
1   teaspoon vanilla
1   teaspoon cornmeal
1   unbaked pie shell

Cream together sugar and margarine. Add eggs one at a time, mixing well after each. Add and stir in vinegar, vanilla and cornmeal. Pour into unbaked pie shell and bake at 350 degrees for 30-45 minutes until "set." Let cool completely before serving. This pie is even better the next day.

Cedar Rock Farm Bed & Breakfast
This charming cottage sits on a 110-acre sheep farm in the beautiful Bluegrass region of Kentucky.

Frankfort, Kentucky
3569 Mink Run Road ~ Frankfort, KY 40601

Chalet Suzanne's Gâteau Christina

Meringue: 4   egg whites
                1½ cups sugar
                ⅓   cup blanched ground almonds

Preheat oven to 250 degrees. Cut aluminum foil into 4-8 inch circles and grease lightly. Whip egg whites until stiff, gradually adding sugar and almonds as eggs begin to stiffen. Place foil rounds on a large baking sheet and spread each evenly with meringue. Bake for 15 minutes or until meringue is dry. Carefully turn meringues over and bake 5 minutes more.

Filling: 2   egg whites
              ½   cup sugar
              2   tablespoons sweetened cocoa
              2   sticks butter, softened
              4   ounces semisweet chocolate, melted

In the top of a double boiler, over hot (not boiling) water, beat egg whites until foamy. Gradually add sugar, cocoa, butter and chocolate, beating until thick and creamy. Remove from heat and cool. Place the best meringue layer on the bottom and spread with chocolate. Top with another meringue, pressing down lightly to make layers fit together. Spread with chocolate. Repeat until all meringues are used and the top is liberally coated with chocolate. Cover and refrigerate for at least 24 hours. Yields one 4-layered gâteau.
Note: These may be stored in tin boxes for gifts.

Chalet Suzanne
This enchanting inn has been operated by the Hinshaw Family since 1931.

Lake Wales, Florida
3800 Chalet Suzanne Dr. ~ Lake Wales, FL 33853-7060 ~ 863-676-6011

Baked Chocolate Pudding

1   pound of chocolate (chopped)
24 eggs (separated)
4   vanilla beans
2   cups sugar
4   cups finely chopped almonds
4   cups fresh bread crumbs

Melt chocolate in a double boiler. Then beat the chocolate with the egg yolks, vanilla and half of the sugar until foamy. Mix the almonds with the bread crumbs. Beat the egg whites with the rest of the sugar until it forms a stiff snow. Blend about ¼ of this snow into the egg yolk mixture and carefully fold in the rest of the egg whites along with the crumb and nut mixture. Fold until totally combined.

Take soufflé dishes and coat them with butter and sugar. Fill the soufflé dishes to the top with the pudding mix. Put them on a sheet pan and fill the sheet pan with water. Place in 350 degree oven until done. Take them out and serve.

Ironrod Chevre Cheesecake with Fresh Berry Confiture

32 ounces goats cheese
16 teaspoons sugar
8   teaspoons cream
8   eggs

Prepare the molds by brushing them lightly with butter and coating them with sugar. Cream together the cheese and sugar. Add the cream and beat until smooth. Beat the eggs with a fork, then whisk it into the cheese mixture until smooth. Fill the molds up ⅛-inch from top.
Place on sheet pan. Fill sheet pan halfway with water. Bake 25 minutes in preheated 325 degree oven. Makes 18 servings.

Fresh Berry Confiture

1 pint strawberries
1 pint blackberries
1 pint raspberries
1 pint blueberries
4 cups of sugar

Place berries in a heavy bottomed saucepan. Add the water and sugar. Stir carefully as not to break up the berries. Bring to a boil, stirring a few times. When the mixture foams up, turn off the heat and let cool.

Clifton The Country Inn
This national registered inn can trace its beginnings back to the Thomas Jefferson family. Fourteen guest rooms are furnished in extraordinary quality and luxury.

Charlottesville, Virginia
1296 Clifton Inn Dr. ~ Charlottesville, VA 22911 ~ 434-971-1800

Cranberries and Cream Bread

3   sticks butter, softened
3   cups sugar
6   eggs
16   ounces sour cream
1   tablespoon vanilla
2   tablespoons grated orange peel or 2 teaspoons orange
     or lemon extract, if desired
6   cups flour
1½   teaspoons baking powder
1   teaspoon soda
1½   teaspoons salt
4   cups whole cranberries

Cream butter and sugar. Add eggs, sour cream, vanilla, orange peel. Add flour, baking powder, soda, salt. Fold in fruit. Pour into 4 greased and floured 4 x 8-inch loaf pans, smoothing over tops, and bake at 350 degrees for 1 hour. (Freezes well)

Colonial Pines
For the nature lover, this inn is nestled among rhododendron, hemlocks, maples and oaks.

Highlands, North Carolina
541 Hickory St. ~ Highlands, NC 28741 ~ 828-526-2060

Carrot Cake

2	cups flour
2	cups sugar
3	cups grated raw carrots
1½	cups vegetable oil
½	cup chopped nuts
4	eggs
2	teaspoons baking powder
2	teaspoons soda
2	teaspoons cinnamon
1	teaspoon salt

Mix oil and sugar. Add eggs, then dry ingredients, then carrots and nuts. Bake in a lightly greased and floured 9 x 11-inch cake pan or two 9-inch pans at 400 degrees for 45 minutes.

Frosting:	8	ounces cream cheese
	1	pound powdered sugar
	2	teaspoons vanilla
	1	stick butter

Mix well and spread on top.

Countryside
This inn captures the spirit of friendliness and old-fashioned hospitality from the moment you step inside.
Summit Point, West Virginia

The Crockett House

Sweet Potato Pie with Brown Sugar and Nutmeg

Crust:
- 2 cups unbleached all purpose flour
- ¼ teaspoon salt
- ⅓ cup chilled solid vegetable shortening, cut into small pieces
- 5 tablespoons chilled unsalted butter, cut into ½-inch pieces
- 6 tablespoons ice water

Combine flour and salt in processor. Add shortening and butter. Using on/off turns, process until mixture resembles coarse meal. Mix in enough water by tablespoonfuls to form moist clumps. Gather dough into ball; flatten into disk. Wrap in plastic; chill until firm enough to roll out, about 1 hour.

Roll out dough on lightly floured surface to generous ⅛-inch thick round. Transfer round to 9-inch-diameter glass pie dish. Trim edge to ¾-inch overhang. Fold overhang under and crimp edge decoratively. Refrigerate while making filling.

Continued on page 106

Southeast Region

Continued from page 107

Filling:	2	large red-skinned sweet potatoes (1¼ to 1½ pounds)
	1	cup (packed) golden brown sugar
	¾	cup whipping cream
	¾	cup orange juice
	3	large eggs
	1	teaspoon vanilla extract
	½	teaspoon salt
	¼	teaspoon ground nutmeg
		Whipped cream

Position rack in bottom third of oven and preheat to 400 degrees. Pierce potatoes with toothpick. Cook in microwave on high until tender, about 6 minutes per side. Cut open and cool completely. Scrape potatoes into processor, discard skins. Blend until smooth. Measure enough sweet potato puree to equal 1½ cups. Reserve remaining puree for another use. Place puree in large bowl. Add brown sugar and next 6 ingredients and whisk until smooth.

Transfer filling to prepared pie crust. Bake until filling puffs around edges and is set in center, about 50 minutes. Transfer to rack; cool completely. Refrigerate until cold, at least 3 hours. (Can be prepared 1 day ahead. Cover and keep refrigerated.)

Serve pie with whipped cream.

The Crockett House

Surrounded by 100-year-old oak trees, pecan and magnolia, this inn dates back to 1895.

Eatonton, Georgia
671 Madison Rd. ~ Eatonton, GA 31024-7830

Cumberland Inn

Crepes al' Flambe

1	egg
¾	cup milk
1	tablespoon butter, melted
1	tablespoon sugar
⅓	cup flour
½	ounce brandy
	salt

Mix all ingredients and blend until smooth. Refrigerate until well chilled. Lightly oil in heavy skillet and heat. Pour 2 tablespoons batter to cover bottom. Cook until underside is brown. Add brandy and sugar.

Cumberland Inn

Superbly located on the edge of Cumberland College campus, this inn is truly the centerpiece of the Cumberland Mountains. The lobby features crystal chandeliers, two grand sweeping staircases and a fresco painted dome full of angels. The ambiance is that of an elegant mansion.

Williamsburg, Kentucky

649 South 10th St. ~ Williamsburg, KY 40769 ~ 606-539-4100

Southeast Region

°D U D L E Y'S°
RESTAURANT

Warm Chocolate Cake

12 ounces bittersweet chocolate
9 ounces butter
6 eggs
6 egg yolks
1½ cups sugar
2 cups flour

Melt chocolate and butter in double boiler. Pour into mixer, add eggs then sugar, scrape sides well with a spatula. Slowly add flour, mix well.
Spray 6-ounce ramekins thoroughly, fill with batter and par bake at 350 degrees until just firm on the top, the center should be uncooked at this point Reheat at 350 degrees for 5 minutes, turn out of ramekins and garnish with fresh raspberries and dust the cake with powdered sugar.

Warm Apple Charlotte

2   tablespoons yeast
4   tablespoons sugar
5   tablespoons salt
2   ounces butter
4   cups milk
12 cups all purpose flour
8   tablespoons brown sugar
4   teaspoons cinnamon

Mix yeast, sugar and salt in large bowl. Melt butter in saucepan. Add milk to heat until warm. Pour warm milk mixture over yeast mixture. Allow to stand for 5 minutes. Stir in flour until the dough begins to come together. Turn onto table and knead until smooth. The dough will be slightly sticky. Add flour if it is really too sticky. Allow the dough to rise in an oiled bowl, covered with a towel until it is doubled in bulk. Punch the dough down and divide into 4 equal pieces. Roll flat and sprinkle with the sugar/cinnamon mixture. Roll the dough up and place in greased loaf pans. Allow to rise until double. Bake at 350 degrees until brown. Tap the loaf, it should sound hollow. Unpan and cool before cutting or freezing. makes about 4 loaves

Cook apples in brandy and sugar until almost a preserve, cut loaves into charlotte shapes, assemble accordingly. Heat charlotte in oven for 3 minutes, top with ice cream and caramel sauce.

Filling: 20 apples, peeled, cored and diced, about 20 cups
           3   cups sugar
           1   tablespoon cinnamon

Cook apples and sugar together until thick and bubbling, like applesauce. Stir in cinnamon.

Grease ramekins liberally with soft butter. Line the ramekins with cinnamon bread, cut to fit. Fill and top with another piece of bread, cut round to fit and cover with butter.

Bake 350 degrees about 30 minutes, until nicely browned and bubbling. Turn out of ramekins. Serve warm with vanilla ice cream, caramel and whipped cream.

Lemon Tart

4   eggs
1½ cups sugar
6   ounces lemon juice
4   ounces butter, melted
    zest of 4 lemons, chopped fine

Mix all ingredients well, pour into prebaked tart shell. Bake at 375 degrees until just set, 15-20 minutes.

Blueberry Compote

1   cup sugar
1   tablespoon lemon juice
¼   cup orange juice
2   cups fresh blueberries

Place sugar, lemon juice and orange juice in a saucepan, bring to a boil then add 1 cup blueberries and cook for 2-3 minutes. Cool mixture then puree in food processor for 20 seconds. Pour mixture into bowl, add remaining blueberries.
Refrigerate in a covered container until needed, makes 1½ cups.

Chocolate Chip Pie

10   eggs
3¾   cups sugar
2   cups flour
1¼   pound butter, melted
2   tablespoons vanilla
2   ounces bourbon
5   cups chocolate chips
5   cups pecans
2   9-inch pie crusts

Combine eggs and sugar. Whip until pale yellow. Add flour, butter, vanilla and bourbon. Combine well. Stir in nuts and chocolate chips. Pour into prebaked pie crust and cover with foil. Bake at 350 degrees for 1½ hours. Remove foil for the final 15 minutes. Let cool and score each pie into 16 pieces. Serve warm with vanilla ice cream or whipped cream.

Dudley's Restaurant

An elementary school from 1851 to the early 30's, now elegant meals are served in the third grade classroom or outside in the warm brick courtyard filled with cozy little tables shaded by smart umbrellas.

Lexington, Kentucky
380 South Mill St. ~ Lexington, KY 40508 ~ 859-252-1010

Southeast Region

Tea Room Scones

2	cups all-purpose flour
2	teaspoons baking powder
½	teaspoon salt
¼	teaspoon baking soda
6	tablespoons butter
½	cup raisins
½	cup buttermilk
1	large egg
1	tablespoon cream or milk
1	tablespoon sugar

Heat oven to 425 degrees. Grease a large baking sheet. Combine the flour, baking powder, salt, and soda. With a pastry blender, cut in the butter until mixture resembles coarse crumbs. Mix in the raisins. Beat together the buttermilk and egg, then add to the flour mixture. Mix lightly until mixture forms a soft dough. Turn out onto a lightly floured surface and knead gently about 5 or 6 times. With a rolling pin, roll the dough to ½ inch thickness. Cut the dough out with a 2-inch cutter and place 1 inch apart on the greased baking sheet. Lightly brush the tops with cream and sprinkle with sugar. Bake for 10-12 minutes or until light golden brown. Serve with lemon curd, preserves or clotted cream.

Elmwood Inn
Gracious hospitality defines this English tea room.

Perryville, Kentucky
205 East Fourth St. ~ Perryville, KY 40468 ~ 859-332-2400

Sweet Memories

Fearrington House

Pear and Fig Brown Butter Tart
with B&B Ice Cream

Shells: 1   package phyllo dough
               4   ounces melted butter
                    powdered sugar

Cut the phyllo dough into 6-inch squares. Brush each sheet with butter and sprinkle with powdered sugar. Stack the squares, alternating them into a star shape. Use five squares per tart. Press the phyllo into 4 ½-inch tart pans. Bake the tart shells at 350 degrees for approximately five minutes, or until golden.

Filling: 6   ounces butter
            3½ ounces blanched almonds mixed with:
            3½ ounces powdered sugar
            2½ ounces all-purpose flour
            6   egg whites
            1   teaspoon vanilla extract
            3½ ounces sugar
            ¼   teaspoon salt

Grind almonds and powdered sugar, until fine. Brown butter in a sauté pan. Set aside to cool. Combine the egg whites, almond/powdered sugar mix, flour, sugar, vanilla and salt in a mixer. Whip together until smooth. Add the cooled brown butter gradually until incorporated. Pour the brown butter filling into the prebaked tart shells. Garnish with peeled, diced pears and halved ripe figs. Bake in a 350 degree oven for approximately 15-20 minutes.

Continued on page 114

Southeast Region

Continued from page 113

Ice Cream: 1   quart heavy cream
           1   vanilla bean
          12 egg yolks
           2   cups milk
         1½ cups sugar
           4   ounces B&B

Bring the cream, milk and vanilla bean (split and scraped) to boil in a heavy saucepan. Remove from heat. Whisk together the egg yolks and sugar. Pour one half of the hot cream into the egg yolks and sugar. Whisk together thoroughly and return all to the half left in the saucepan. Return to the heat and stir constantly, cooking until mixture thickly coats a spoon. DO NOT BOIL. Remove from heat, strain and chill. Ad the B&B and freeze in an ice cream maker according to manufacturer's instructions.

Sauce: 1½ cups sugar
           2   cups cream
           1   cup corn syrup
           4   ounces butter

Bring the sugar and corn syrup to a boil in a heavy saucepan. Continue to boil, until the sugar turns the color of iced tea. Carefully add the cream and return to a boil. Remove from heat and add the butter.

Pool caramel sauce on a plate. Place the warm tart onto the sauce and top with a scoop of ice cream. Drizzle with caramel sauce. Serves 12.

Fearrington House
Once a dairy farm, it has welcomed visitors since 1986.

Pittsboro, North Carolina
2000 Fearrington Village Ctr. ~ Pittsboro, NC 27312-8502 ~ 919-542-2121

Snug Hollow Farm

Chocolate Pie

1	scant cup honey
5	level tablespoons flour
3	squares unsweetened chocolate, cut up
¼	teaspoon salt
2⅓	cups evaporated milk
3	egg yolks, slightly beaten
1	teaspoon vanilla extract
½	teaspoon maple flavoring
2	tablespoons butter
Meringue: 3	egg whites at room temperature
¼	teaspoon cream of tartar
6	tablespoons sugar
	drop of maple flavoring

Preheat oven to 400 degrees. Prepare and bake a pie shell. In medium saucepan, combine honey, flour, chocolate and salt. Mix well. Gradually stir in milk, mixing until smooth. Bring mixture to a boil over medium heat. Boil for one minute, stirring constantly. Remove from heat. Stir half of mixture into egg yolks and mix well. Pour into saucepan. Bring back to boiling while stirring; boil one minute. Remove from heat, add butter. Stir in extracts and pour into pie shell.

Make meringue: in a medium bowl, beat egg whites and cream of tartar at medium until peaks form. Gradually beat in sugar, 2 tablespoons at a time. Add maple and beat until stiff peaks form. Spread meringue over warm filling, sealing edges of crust. Bake 7-10 minutes or until meringue is golden. Cool.

Snug Hollow Farm

790 McSwain Branch (located on Highway 594) ~ Irvine, KY 40336 ~ 606-723-4786

Southeast Region

Buttermilk Pie

1   unbaked pie shell
1½   cups sugar
1   teaspoon butter flavor
¼   cup butter, melted and cooled
4   eggs
½   cup buttermilk
1   teaspoon vanilla

Beat eggs and sugar until fluffy. Add buttermilk and butter, mixing well. Stir in flavorings. Pour in shell. Bake on lower shelf at 375 degrees 45 minutes or until center is almost set but still soft. Cool thoroughly before slicing.

Fryemont Inn
This national landmark was built in 1923 by local craftsmen using the finest oak, chestnut and maple to be found anywhere.

Bryson City, North Carolina
245 Fryemont St. ~ P.O. Box 459 ~ Bryson City, NC 28713 ~ 828-488-2159

The Garden and the Sea Inn

Chocolate Pecan Pie

3   cups pecans, coarsely chopped
2½ cups semisweet chocolate chips
1   cup firmly packed brown sugar
1   cup light corn syrup
½   cup unsalted butter, softened
4   extra-large eggs
4   teaspoons vanilla extract
2   9-inch pie shells

Sprinkle pecans and chocolate chips evenly over the pie crust. In a small bowl, beat together the butter, corn syrup, brown sugar, eggs and vanilla until smooth. Pour slowly and evenly over the nuts and chips so as not to disturb them. Bake at 325 degrees until slightly firm, about 50 minutes. Transfer to a wire rack to cool completely. Serve at room temperature.

The Garden and the Sea Inn
This is an outdoorsman's paradise and home to the world famous wild ponies.

New Church, Virginia
4188 Nelson Rd. ~ P.O. Box 275 ~ New Church, VA 23415-0275 ~ 800-824-0672

Glenn Ella Springs Inn

Apple Bread Pudding with Cinnamon Ice Cream

2	cups Granny Smith apples, peeled and chopped
¼	cup apple schnapps
½	cup light brown sugar
4	cups stale biscuits or coarse bread, crumbled
¼	cup raisins
¼	cup diced dried apricots
¼	cup diced dried dates
2	cups butterscotch sauce, purchased or made
8	scoops cinnamon ice cream, see recipe

Preheat oven to 375. In small shallow pan, combine apples with brown sugar and schnapps, bake until sugar melts and apples are tender: 15-20 minutes. Set aside to cool. Toss apples with crumbled bread and dried fruits and place in a well-greased 8-inch baking pan or shallow casserole.

Custard:	2	cups half and half
	3	eggs, slightly beaten
	1	tablespoon pure vanilla extract
	⅔	cup sugar

Combine all ingredients and pour over bread. Bake for approximately 45 minutes until custard is set and golden brown.

Serve warm. To serve, cut into squares, place each square in a shallow bowl, top with a scoop of cinnamon ice cream and warm butterscotch sauce.

If preparing in advance, store in refrigerator. Wrap in foil to rewarm, or place individual servings in microwave for a few seconds. May also be frozen, thaw before heating.

Ice Cream:

½ gallon vanilla ice cream (premium brand), softened
1 tablespoon ground cinnamon
3 tablespoons sugar
2 tablespoons apple schnapps

Place ice cream in large bowl of mixer, beat on low speed until softened, add other ingredients. Mix to combine thoroughly and refreeze.

Glenn Ella Springs Inn
Double porches and rocking chairs lend tranquility to this charming retreat.

Clarksville, Georgia
1789 Bear Gap Rd. ~ Clarksville, GA 30523 ~ 706-754-1560

Graves Mountain Lodge

Fruit Cream Pie

10	ounces blueberries, peaches, or strawberries
8	ounces cream cheese
1	cup whipped topping
1	9-inch baked pie shell
1	cup confectioners sugar
	pecans, chopped

Heat oven to 400 degrees. Cover bottom of pie shell with pecans and bake until brown. Cool. Blend cream cheese and confectioners sugar. Fold in whipped topping and fruit. Pour into cooled pie shell and chill. Top with additional whipped topping before serving.

Graves Mountain Lodge
This inn prizes itself on southern hospitality and good food.

Syria, Virginia
3853 Old Blue Ridge Turnpike, Rt. 670 ~ Syria, VA 22743-9999 ~ 540-923-4231

Greystone's Russian Cream with Brandy Berries

Cream:	2½	cups heavy cream
	1	cup sugar
	1½	tablespoons unflavored gelatin
	2	cups sour cream
	1	tablespoon vanilla
	8	sprigs fresh mint

Sprinkle gelatin over the heavy cream and allow to bloom, approximately 5 minutes. Add sugar and heat over a double boiler until the sugar and gelatin have melted. Add sour cream and vanilla. Pour mixture into 4-ounce molds and refrigerate.

Berries:	3	pints mixed berries
	½	cup sugar
	½	cup brandy

Wash and pick through the berries thoroughly. Bruise about 25 percent of the berries and add the sugar and brandy. Add the remaining berries, refrigerate and allow to set approximately 4 hours for the flavors to blend. Remove Russian cream from the mold, spoon the berries over the mold and serve. Garnish with whole strawberry and fresh mint.

Southeast Region

Greystone Inn's Double Buttermilk Pie

Crust: 2   cups Graham Cracker crumbs
            ½   cup melted butter

Mix ingredients together. In a 9-inch spring form pan, press mixture into the bottom and sides.

Filling: 8   large eggs
          2   cups buttermilk
          ½   cup heavy cream
          1   cup sour cream
          1   tablespoon vanilla
          3   cups granulated sugar
          1   pound cream cheese

Cream the cream cheese and sugar together until smooth. Add sour cream and blend until smooth. Add eggs one at a time and mix well. Add heavy cream, buttermilk and vanilla.

Slowly pour mixture into crust. Bake at 350 degrees for one hour and fifteen minutes. Check doneness by inserting a wooden skewer into the center of the pie: it should come out clean. Allow to cool for one hour and remove from pan.

Greystone Inn
A 4-diamond inn surrounded by the beautiful Blue Ridge Mountains.

Lake Toxaway, North Carolina
Greystone Lane ~ Lake Toxaway, NC 28747 ~ 828-966-4700

High Hampton Inn

Black Bottom Pie

1½ cups crushed Zwieback
¼   cup powdered sugar
6   tablespoons melted butter
1   teaspoon cinnamon

Mix ingredients well and place in pie pan, patting along sides and bottom to make crust. Bake in moderate oven 15 minutes.

1	tablespoon gelatin
2	cups rich milk
4	egg yolks, beaten lightly
1½	ounces melted chocolate
1	cup sugar
4	teaspoons cornstarch
½	teaspoon vanilla
1	teaspoon almond flavoring
3	egg whites
¼	teaspoon salt
¼	cup sugar
¼	teaspoon cream of tartar

Soak gelatin in ½ cup cold water. Scald milk. Combine egg yolks, 1 cup sugar, and cornstarch. Stir in gradually milk and cook over hot water until custard will coat a spoon. Take out 1 cup custard and add chocolate to it. Beat until well blended and cool. Add vanilla and pour into pie shell. Dissolve gelatin in remaining custard, cool, but do not permit to stiffen, stirring in almond flavoring, egg whites, salt, ¼ cup sugar, cream of tartar. Beat egg whites and salt until blended, add cream of tartar and beat until stiff, gradually adding sugar, folding in remaining custard and covering chocolate custard with almond-flavored custard. Chill and set. Whip cup of heavy cream. Add 2 tablespoons powdered sugar and spread over pie.

High Hampton Inn
All sports abound at this rustic resort that stands at an altitude of 3,600 feet.

South Cashiers, North Crolina
1525 Highway 107 ~ South Cashiers, NC 28717 ~ 828-743-2411

Grey Gables Bed & Breakfast Inn

Chess Cake

1	1-pound box light brown sugar
½	cup granulated sugar
2	sticks butter, melted
4	eggs
2	cups flour
1	teaspoon baking powder
½	teaspoon salt
1	teaspoon vanilla

Combine sugars, melted butter and eggs, one at a time, beating at medium mixer speed after each addition. Sift flour with baking powder and salt, and add to creamed mixture. Add vanilla. Pour batter into well-greased 9 x 13-inch pan. Bake at 300 degrees for about 45 minutes. Cut into squares when cool and roll in powdered sugar.

Hickory Nut Cake

1   cup butter
2   cups powdered sugar
    grated rind of 1 lemon
4   eggs, separated
3   cups sifted flour
2   teaspoons baking powder
1   cup milk
1   pint hickory nuts

Wash butter in cold water. Place in bowl and add powdered sugar. Beat until light creamy white. Add lemon rind, stirring constantly. Add egg yolks. Add sifted flour and baking powder alternately with milk to creamed mixture. Fold in stiffly beaten egg whites. Dust chopped hickory nuts with flour and fold into batter. Butter zinc loaf cake pan and dust with flour. Pour in batter and bake in slow oven for approximately 1 hour. (This recipe appeared in "The Brooklyn Eagle" in 1987.)

Sun Gold Cake

2   cups sugar
1   cup butter
4   eggs
1   cup milk
3   cups flour
3   teaspoons baking powder
1   teaspoon vanilla
    pinch of salt

Cream sugar and butter. Add egg yolks. Sift flour and baking powder and add with the milk. Add vanilla and salt. Fold in stiffly beaten egg whites. Bake in 350 degree oven. Makes 3 layers. Frost with your favorite icing.

Buttermilk Coconut Pie

¼   cup butter or margarine
1   cup sugar
2   tablespoons all-purpose flour
    dash of salt
4   eggs, beaten lightly
1   cup buttermilk
2   teaspoons vanilla extract
1   cup grated coconut

Melt butter or margarine. Remove from heat; stir in sugar, flour and salt. Add beaten eggs, vanilla and buttermilk; stir till well blended. Stir in coconut. Pour into unbaked pie shell. Bake in 350 degree oven approximately 45 minutes, or until set and lightly browned.

Pecan Pie

¼   pound butter
1½   cups brown sugar (light)
5   whole eggs
1½   cups red label Karo syrup
1   teaspoon vanilla
¾   cup pecans (chopped)

Cream butter and sugar. Beat eggs and add to butter and sugar, beat well. Add Karo syrup and vanilla. Pour in large pie plate lined with crust. Sprinkle with pecans. Bake 10 minutes at 450 degrees, reduce heat to 300 degrees and continue baking until done, about 1 hour. Test center with silver knife. This makes 1 large or 2 small pies and is best served with real whipped cream.

Southeast Region

Carrot Cake 1

2   cups sugar
2   cups sifted flour
2   teaspoons baking soda
½   teaspoon salt
2   teaspoons cinnamon
¼   teaspoon allspice
4   eggs
1½   cups cooking oil
1   cup finely chopped nuts
1   cup chopped raisins
3   cups grated raw carrots

Beat eggs and oil together. Mix in sugar. Mix in combined dry ingredients. Stir in nuts, raisins and carrots. Grease and flour 9 x 13-inch pan and pour in batter. Bake at 325 degrees for approximately 45 minutes. When cool, top with favorite frosting. Cut in squares.

Carrot Cake 2

2   cups flour
2   cups sugar
3   teaspoons cinnamon
2   teaspoons baking soda
1   teaspoon salt
4   well-beaten eggs
1½   cups vegetable oil
3   cups grated raw carrots

Sift dry ingredients together. Add eggs, oil, and grated carrots and mix at medium speed. Pour into two greased and floured cake pans. Bake at 350 degrees for 35 minutes.

Sweet Potato Custard Pie

Pastry for two 8-inch pies
2½ cups mashed sweet potatoes
½   teaspoon salt
2   cups milk
4   tablespoons butter
3   tablespoons flour
2   cups sugar
4   eggs
2   teaspoons vanilla

Cook sweet potatoes in jackets until tender. Skin and put through colander while hot. Add salt and mix. Simmer milk with butter. Mix flour and sugar and add to hot milk. Beat eggs until frothy and add to milk. Add mashed sweet potatoes and stir until mixture begins to bubble. Add vanilla. Pour into pastry shells; sprinkle top with nutmeg and brown sugar. Bake in 400 degree oven for 10 minutes; reduce to 350 degrees and bake until custard is firm and lightly browned, usually 30-40 minutes.

Grey Gables Bed & Breakfast Inn
Founded in 1880 by noted English author/social reformer Thomas Hughes, twenty Victorian buildings still stand in this once utopian community in Appalachia.
Rugby, Tennessee
Hwy 52, P.O. Box 52 ~ Rugby, TN 37733 ~ 423-628-5252

The Inn at Gristmill Square

Grand Marnier Soufflé

2	cups sugar
1	cup water
1	cup Grand Marnier
1½	quarts whipping cream
18	egg yolks
½	cup sifted powdered sugar
1	tablespoon vanilla

Combine 2 cups sugar with water and bring to a boil. Whip egg yolks until pale yellow ribbons form, and add powdered sugar. Slowly mix sugar water into eggs, and add Grand Marnier and Vanilla. Beat whipping cream until stiff and fold into mixture.

Put mixture into 25 serving goblets and place in freezer until firm. Serve with a dab of whipped cream and grated orange rind on top.

The Inn at Gristmill Square
A cluster of five delightful buildings, one of which dates back to 1771.

Warm Springs, Virginia
Rte. 645-Old Mill Rd. ~ PO Box 359 ~ Warm Springs, VA 24484-0359 ~ 540-839-2231

The Joshua Wilton House
Inn and Restaurant

Peach Ice Cream Served in a Grilled Peach with Raspberry and Almond Slices

Fruit: 1½ cup peaches, roughly sliced
           ⅞   cup sugar, vary according to ripeness of fruit
           1   tablespoon lemon juice

Combine all ingredients in a bowl and allow to macerate overnight in the refrigerator, stirring occasionally. Strain syrup into small saucepan and reduce by half. Add peaches and cook until soft enough to puree. Do not overcook. Puree and pass through a strainer.

Ice Cream: 1   cup heavy cream
              1   cup half and half
              4   large egg yolks
              1   tablespoon Amaretto

Warm the cream and half and half to just below a boil. Gently whisk the egg yolks together. Temper the yolks with about ¼ cup of the warm cream mixture. Add the yolks into the rest of the cream and cook until thick enough to coat the back of a spoon or until it reaches 170 degrees. Cool to 40 degrees and add peach puree. Freeze in ice cream maker according to manufacturer's instructions.

Continued on page 132

131   *Southeast Region*

Continued from page 131

Sauces
Raspberry: 1   cup sugar
           1   cup water
           2   pints fresh or frozen raspberries

Combine the water and sugar and boil to the soft ball stage. Add berries and bring to a boil. Remove from heat and puree. Pass through a strainer to remove seeds. Chill.

Almond: 2   cups half and half
           ½   cup sugar
           4   egg yolks
           ½   teaspoon almond extract, or:
           2   tablespoons Amaretto

Scald cream. Whisk sugar into yolks and add warm cream slowly. Cook over very low heat, stirring constantly until thick. Strain and add flavoring. Chill.

To assemble:
Cut peaches in half and brush lightly with a flavorless oil. Grill over low heat until warmed through, but still holds shape. Swirl sauces together on plates. Top with peach half and top each peach half with ice cream. Serve immediately.

The Joshua Wilton House Inn and Restaurant
This Victorian Inn dates back 110 years.
Harrisburg, Virginia
412 South Main St ~ Harrisonburg, VA 22801 ~ 888-294-5866

L'Auberge Provençale

Chocolate Mousse

10 ounces chocolate squares
⅛ teaspoon salt
3 ounces Amaretto
10 egg yolks
10 egg whites
10 teaspoons confectioners sugar
1 teaspoon vanilla
1 pint heavy cream
5 teaspoons confectioners sugar
1 teaspoon vanilla

Heat chocolate, Amaretto, salt in double boiler. Beat mixture into well beaten egg yolks. Add whipped cream into chocolate mixture. Fold beaten egg whites into pudding. Pipe into champagne glass.

Chocolate Chip Fudge Cake

6 ounces unsalted butter
6 ounces unsweetened chocolate
6 eggs
3 cups sugar
½ teaspoon salt
2 teaspoons vanilla extract
1½ cups flour
1½ cups chocolate chips

Melt butter and chocolate in double boiler. Whisk eggs, sugar, salt, vanilla to combine. Stir in flour, chocolate chips and chocolate mixture. Pour into 9 x 1½ inch pans that have been greased and floured. Bake at 350 degrees for 30-40 minutes.

Southeast Region

Amaretto Cheesecake

Crust: 1   cup graham cracker crumbs
            ½   cup sugar
            4   tablespoons butter (melted)

Filling: 2½   pounds cream cheese
            ¾   cup sugar
            3   eggs
            2   tablespoons Amaretto
            1   teaspoon almond extract
            1   ounce lime juice

Topping: 2   cups sour cream
            ½   cup sugar
            ½   teaspoon vanilla

Mix cream cheese and sugar. Add lime juice, almond extract and Amaretto. Add eggs and beat well. Pour into ¼ inch thick crust, baked 10 minutes at 350. Bake at 350 for 30 minutes. Cool. Mix sour cream, sugar and vanilla. Spoon over top of cake. Bake 350 for 10 minutes. Refrigerate overnight.

Sweet Cream with Basil Compote

2   packages gelatin
6   tablespoons cold water
3   cups heavy whipping cream
1½   cups sugar
4½   ounces crème fraiche
9   ounces cream cheese
4½   teaspoons vanilla extract
3   tablespoons freshly squeezed lemon juice

In small bowl, sprinkle the gelatin over cold water and let stand for 10 minutes. Whisk together the heavy cream, sugar, cream fraiche and cream cheese in large stainless steel bowl and place over a pot of simmering water. When cream mixture is warm and cream cheese has dissolved, dissolve the gelatin over low heat and add to cream mixture. Remove from heat, stir in vanilla extract and lemon juice. Strain the custard through a fine strainer. Pour cream into ramekins of 4 ounces and refrigerate for several hours. Serves 15 to 18.

Peach Basil Compote

1   cup coarsely chopped basil
8   cups slice peaches
6   cups water
2   cups sugar
2   cups raspberries
2   cups strawberries slices
2   cups blackberries

Bring to boil the water, sugar, add peaches and broil. Cook on low until peaches become soft. Remove from heat. Cool.

Place sweet cream in bowl by taking a knife and run round edge of ramekin and dip in warm water to loosen ladle 3 ounces of peach basil compote into bowl with cream. Add assorted berries around cream in peach compote and garnish with purple or African basil.

L'Auberge Provençale
Truly like an inn in the south of France, where expectations are quietly met.

White Post, Virginia
P.O. Box 190 ~ White Post, VA 22663 ~ 540-837-1375

Southeast Region

Key Lime Napoleon with Fresh Tropical Fruit

9 egg yolks
3 large eggs
1 cup sugar
1 cup key lime juice
½ pound butter

Add all ingredients together except for butter. Stir over water bath until thick. Whisk in butter until incorporated. Cover with plastic wrap and chill for approximately 12 hours. Then when serving fold in equal portion unsugared and unflavored whip cream and add mixture of chopped fresh tropical fruit.

Phyllo Triangles

4   sheets phyllo dough
½   cup melted butter
½   cup sugar
1   cup raw finely ground macadamia nuts

Brush first sheet of phyllo with butter, sprinkle well with sugar and one-third the ground nuts. Cover with second sheet of phyllo. Pat down. Repeat butter, sugar and nut procedure. Repeat with third phyllo sheet. Place fourth sheet of phyllo on top, pat down, butter and sugar only.
Using a pizza cutter, cut evenly into 8 rectangles, then cut each rectangle in half, thus creating 16 triangles.
Using a thin spatula, transfer the triangles to a parchment lined sheet pan. Cover with parchment paper and a second sheet pan. Bake at 375 degrees 10 to 12 minutes until golden.

Marquesa Hotel
A 27-room luxury hotel in Old Town, Key West.

Key West, Florida
600 Fleming St. ~ Key West, FL 33040 ~ 305-292-1919

Southeast Region

Peanut Butter Custard

Pie Shell: 3   cups flour
                 1   part water
                 1   part shortening
                     pinch salt

Mix and roll lightly.
NOTE: You may also use one pre-made 9-inch pie shell.

Filling: 1   cup peanut butter
               1½ cups granulated sugar
               2   eggs
               1   teaspoon real vanilla
               ½   teaspoon salt
               1½ cups milk or cream

On low speed, blend peanut butter and vanilla, then add sugar and salt. Add eggs, using medium speed, then add milk on low speed. Mix to smooth. Bake 45-50 minutes at 375 degrees.

The Martha Washington Inn
This fabulous repository of our nation's history is both a museum and an inn with great charm and beauty.

Abingdon, Virginia
150 West Main St. ~ Abingdon, VA 24210 ~ 276-628-3161

Sweet Memories

Banana Pound Cake

1	cup shortening
½	cup butter, softened
3	cups sugar
5	large eggs
3	ripe bananas, mashed
3	tablespoons milk
2	teaspoons vanilla extract
3	cups all-purpose flour
½	teaspoon salt
1	teaspoon baking powder

Beat shortening and butter at medium speed with an electric mixer about 3 minutes or until creamy. Gradually add sugar, beating 5 to 7 minutes. Add egg, one at a time, beating just until yellow disappears. Combine mashed bananas, milk and vanilla. Combine flour, salt and baking powder; add to shortening mixture alternately with banana mixture, beginning and ending with flour mixture. Beat at low speed just until blended after each addition. Pour batter into a greased and floured 10-inch tube pan. Bake at 350 degrees for one hour and 20 minutes, or until a wooden pick inserted in the center of the cake comes out clean. Cool in pan on wire rack 10 to 15 minutes; remove cake from pan and let cool completely on wire rack.

Miss Betty's Bed & Breakfast Inn
Selected as "one of the best places to stay in the South," this charming inn dates back to 1858 when built as a home.

600 West Nash St. ~ Wilson, NC 27893 ~ 252-243-4447

Fudge-N-Crème Pie

½   cup melted butter
3   tablespoons cocoa
¾   cup hot water
2   cups granulated sugar
⅛   teaspoon salt
½   cup plain flour
2   eggs
1   cup condensed milk
1   teaspoon vanilla

Pour into 9-inch unbaked pie shell. Bake 375 degrees approximately 1 hour. Cool.

Topping: ¼   cup melted butter
            8   large tablespoons powdered sugar
                 pinch salt
                 a little cream or milk

Fresh Apple Cake

¾   cup oil
3   cups chopped apples
1   teaspoon salt
1   teaspoon soda
1   teaspoon cinnamon
2   cups sugar
2   cups all-purpose flour
1   teaspoon vanilla
1   cup chopped nuts
1   egg

Mix oil, apples and sugar and set aside. Mix all other ingredients and add to apple mixture. Bake at 350 degrees for 40-45 minutes. Cool.

Topping: ½   cup butterscotch chips
6   tablespoons margarine
¾   cup brown sugar
½   cup evaporated milk
1   cup coconut
1   tablespoon vanilla
1   cup chopped nuts

Mix all ingredients, pour over cake after cooled and broil until golden.

Mountain View Inn
Romantic and comfortable in beautiful Smoky Mountains.

Gatlinburg, Tennessee
P.O. Box 707 ~ Gatlinburg, TN 37738-0707 ~ 865-436-5761

Old Talbott Tavern

Chess Pie

1½ cups sugar
¼   cup margarine
¾   cup milk
3   eggs
1   teaspoon vanilla
1   tablespoon flour
1   pie shell
    pinch of salt

Mix all ingredients thoroughly and pour into pie shell; bake at 375 degrees for 1 hour and 15 minutes. Makes one pie.

Old Talbott Tavern
Old Talbott Tavern was licensed under Patrick Henry and has welcomed guests to Bardstown since 1779.

Bardstown, Kentucky
107 West Stephen Foster ~ Bardstown, KY 40004 ~ 502-348-3494

Richmond Hill Inn

Strawberry Napoleons

Grand Marnier Sabayon
Puff Pastries
Raspberry Sauce
4¼ cups fresh strawberries
2   tablespoons granulated sugar
1   teaspoon Framboise liqueur
3   tablespoons confectioner's sugar

Sabayon: 8   large egg yolks
          ½   cup granulated sugar
          ½   cup Grand Marnier liqueur
          ½   cup fresh orange juice
          1   cup heavy whipping cream
              pinch salt

In a large stainless steel bowl, combine the egg yolks, sugar, and salt. Whisk in the liqueur and orange juice and set aside. Fill a large bowl one quarter full of ice water and set aside. Place the reserved stainless steel bowl over a pot of boiling water and whisk the egg mixture vigorously for 5 minutes or until thick and tripled in volume. (The sabayon should mound slightly when dropped from the whisk.) Immediately put the stainless steel bowl over the reserved bowl of ice and whisk until cold. Pour the whipping cream into another large bowl and with an electric mixer at high speed, whip until soft peaks form. Fold the whipped cream into the sabayon and chill until ready to serve. Makes 5 cups.

Continued on page 144

Southeast Region

Continued from page 143

Pastry:
    1   **pound cold sweet butter**
    2½ **cups all-purpose flour**
    ½   **cup ice-cold water**
    ½   **teaspoon salt**

Combine 2 cups of the flour and the salt on the work surface. Cut the butter into ¼-inch cubes. Toss the butter with the flour mixture so that all of the cubes are coated well. Shape the mixture into a mound and make a well in the center.

Pour the water into the well and with fingertips work in the water so that a rough dough begins to form. (It will look like torn and knotted rags.) Gently press the dough together so that all of the dry flour is absorbed. Form this dough into a rectangle about 6 x 8 x 1¼-inches thick. Carefully wrap the dough in plastic wrap and chill for 1 hour.

Roll out the chilled dough on a lightly floured surface into a rectangle about 7 x 16 x ½-inch thick. (If the butter is breaking through the flour, let the dough sit out for 5 minutes at room temperature before attempting to roll it.) With the short end of the dough closest to you, bring the top down ⅔ of the way and fold the bottom over the top. This is a single turn.

Give the dough a quarter turn so that the open seam is on your right and the closed seam on your left. Repeat the rolling and folding process, giving the dough another single turn. Carefully wrap the dough in plastic wrap and chill for 1 hour. Give the chilled dough two more single turns, rolling and folding, and making sure to give it a quarter turn between single turns. Rewrap the dough and chill for 1 hour more.

Again give the chilled dough two single turns, rolling and folding. Rewrap again and chill for 1 hour to overnight before rolling to desired thickness. Makes ten 5 x 5 x ⅛-inch thick pieces or twenty 4 x 5 x 1/16-inch thick pieces. (The pastry can be frozen for later use.)

Tips for rolling puff pastry:

Place the pastry on a floured surface. Sprinkle flour on top and roll to the thickness specified in the recipe. Keep the edges of the puff pastry straight and even as you roll. Occasionally sprinkle flour underneath and on top to prevent the pastry from sticking.

Brush off excess flour. Cut the pastry by pressing a knife down with a rocking motion to make a clean cut. Do not drag the knife through the pastry. Freeze pastry pieces until ready to use.

To create the traditional mille-feuille (1,000 layers) for napoleons, pierce holes with the tines of a fork all over the pastry. (This is called docking and prevents the dough from rising.) Place an inverted wire mesh cooling rack over the pastry when baking to further prevent it from rising.

Sauce:

1	pint fresh raspberries
2	tablespoons granulated sugar
½	teaspoon fresh lemon juice
	pinch salt

In a food processor, puree the raspberries. Strain the puree through a medium-mesh sieve to eliminate any remaining seeds.
Stir in the sugar, lemon juice and salt. Taste and adjust for sweetness. Chill until ready to use. Makes 1 cup.

Assembly:
On a lightly floured surface, roll the pastry to ⅟₁₆-inch thick. Dock the pastry. (To dock the pastry, pierce holes with the tines of a fork all over the surface of the pastry.) Cut into 12 pieces, each 4 x 5-inches. Freeze the pastry for at least 1 hour.
Preheat oven to 375 degrees. Line two baking sheets with parchment paper and place the frozen pastry on the sheets. Cover with inverted wire mesh cooling racks and bake for 15-20 minutes or until golden brown.
In a medium-sized bowl, toss together the strawberries, sugar, and liqueur. Put one piece of pastry on each of six plates. Spoon on some of the berry mixture and then some of the sabayon. Drizzle on the raspberry sauce. Sprinkle the remaining six pieces of pastry with the confectioner's sugar and place on top. Serves 6.

Maple Pecan Scones

3   cups all-purpose flour
1½ tablespoons baking powder
¾   teaspoon salt
¾   cup unsalted butter, chilled and cut into 12 pieces
1   cup chopped pecans
⅓   cup milk
⅔   cup maple syrup, plus 2 tablespoons for brushing
      tops of scones

Preheat oven to 350 degrees. Grease and flour a cookie sheet. In a large bowl, sift together the flour, baking powder and salt. Cut the butter into the sifted dry ingredients using a pastry blender or two table knives. Add the chopped pecans to the mixture. Whisk together the milk and maple syrup. Pour over the dry ingredients and mix lightly until combined. Roll out dough on a floured surface to a thickness of 1½ inches. Cut scones using a 3-inch round cutter. Place on prepared cookie sheet, brush the tops of the scones with the reserved maple syrup and bake for 15 to 20 minutes or until golden. Makes 12.

Swiss Chocolate Cherries Jubilee

1   16-ounce can pitted bing cherries in syrup
6   tablespoons kirsch (cherry brandy) or cognac
¾   cup heavy cream
4   ounces bittersweet chocolate, chopped
¼   cup red currant jelly
¼   cup creme de cassis (black currant liqueur) or other
     liqueur
1   quart vanilla ice cream

Drain the cherries well, reserving two tablespoons of the syrup. Put the cherries in a bowl and add the kirsch. Let sit for at least one hour to allow the cherries to absorb the flavor of the liqueur. Make a chocolate topping: in a saucepan, heat the cream to a simmer. Process the chocolate in a food processor until very finely ground. With the motor running, pour the hot cream through the feed tube onto the chocolate. The chocolate topping should be very smooth.

In a small saucepan, heat the red currant jelly, creme de cassis and the reserved two tablespoons of cherry syrup. Stir until the mixture is smooth. Set aside. Drain the cherries, reserving the kirsch. In a sauté pan over medium heat, cook the cherries and two tablespoons of the reserved kirsch for about one minute. Add the red currant jelly sauce and cook, stirring constantly, until the mixture bubbles. Reduce heat to low.

In a large ladle or small saucepan, carefully warm the remaining kirsch over low heat. Ignite the kirsch and pour it over the cherries, shaking the pan until the flame subsides. Divide the ice cream between eight stemmed glasses. Spoon two tablespoons of the warm chocolate topping over the ice cream and top with the hot cherries. Serves 8.

Southeast Region

Bread Pudding with Bourbon Sauce

Pudding:
- 4   eggs
- 2¼   cups half and half
- ¾   cup sugar
- 1   tablespoon vanilla
- 4   cups cubed French bread (stale bread works best)
- ⅓   cup dried fruit (golden raisins, dried cranberries or cherries, chopped dried apricots)
- ⅓   cup chopped walnuts or pecans

Preheat oven to 350 degrees. In a large mixing bowl, lightly beat the eggs. Add the half and half, sugar and vanilla. Toss the bread, dried fruit and chopped nuts in a 8 x 8 x 2-inch baking dish. Pour the egg mixture over and stir gently to coat the bread thoroughly. Bake for 40 to 45 minutes or until knife inserted near center comes out clean. Serve warm with bourbon sauce.

Sauce:
- ¼   cup butter, melted and cooled
- ½   cup sugar
- 1   egg yolk, lightly beaten
- 2   tablespoons water
- 2   tablespoons bourbon

In a small saucepan, combine the melted butter, sugar, beaten egg yolk and water. Cook, stirring constantly, over medium-low heat for 4 to 5 minutes or until sugar dissolves and mixture just begins to bubble. Remove from heat. Stir in bourbon.

Richmond Hill Inn
This national registered landmark with its distinctive gables, turrets and bays is an outstanding example of the Ocean Annie-style architecture.

Asheville, North Carolina
87 Richmond Hill Dr. ~ Asheville, NC 28806 ~ 828-252-7313

The Sanderling

Chocolate Pecan Pie with Bourbon Ice Cream

¾ cup packed brown sugar
6 tablespoons butter
¾ cup light corn syrup
3 eggs
1 tablespoon bourbon
1 teaspoon vanilla extract
1½ cups pecans
1 cup chocolate chips
1 9-inch unbaked pie crust

Place the brown sugar in a mixing bowl. Melt the butter and add it to the sugar. With a whisk, combine. Add the corn syrup and mix well. In a separate bowl, slightly beat the eggs. Add them to the brown sugar mixture and mix well. Pour the pecans and chocolate chips into the filling mixture and stir to mix evenly. Pour into the pie shell. Bake at 350 degrees for 45 minutes or until the filling is set.

Continued on page 150

Southeast Region

Continued from page 149

Ice Cream: 1   cup heavy cream
            6   egg yolks
            ¼   cup Jim Beam
            ¼   cup sugar
            1   teaspoon vanilla extract
            2   cups half-and-half

In a saucepan, heat the heavy cream and slightly more than half the bourbon to a simmer. When you begin to see steam, whisk the yolks and sugar together in a small bowl. Pour a small amount of the cream into the yolks and quickly whisk to combine. Gradually add the yolks to the simmering cream whisking constantly. Continue to cook, whisking continuously, until the cream mixture is thickened slightly. Remove from the heat and add the half-and-half, vanilla and the remaining bourbon. Cool and then freeze according to your manufacturer's instructions.

Triple Chocolate Cheesecake

Crust: 1   cup Oreo cookie crumbs
                4   tablespoons butter (approximately)

Melt the butter and mix with the cookie crumbs. Press down in the base of a 9-inch springform pan.

Filling: 26   ounces cream cheese, softened
              1   cup sugar
              ¼   cup cornstarch
              3   eggs
              2   egg yolks
              ⅓   cup heavy cream
             12   ounces semisweet chocolate, melted and cooled

In the bowl of a tabletop mixer, place the cream cheese, cornstarch, and sugar. Beat until well combined, scraping the sides of the bowl frequently. Gradually add the eggs and yolks, scraping after each addition. On low speed add the heavy cream. When combined, add the chocolate and mix well. Scrape the bowl often. Pour the filling into the springform pan and place in a baking dish. Fill halfway up the sides of the pan with hot water. Cover and place in the 325 degree oven. Bake 1½-2 hours or until the center of the cake is set. Remove from the oven and let cool a few minutes at room temperature before placing in the refrigerator to chill overnight.

Topping: 3   ounces white chocolate, chopped
              2   tablespoons heavy cream

Heat the cream in a small saucepan until it just starts to boil. Pour over the white chocolate and let stand 5 minutes. Then stir to combine. Remove the sides of the springform pan and pour the white chocolate over the cooled cheesecake. Let set and serve.

The Sanderling Inn Resort
Open all year with good food and lodging.

Duck, North Carolina
1461 Duck Rd. ~ Duck, NC 27949 ~ 800-701-4111

Southeast Region

Shaker Village at Pleasant Hill

Bread Pudding

4	cups stale bread, about
¼	teaspoon salt
1	teaspoon vanilla
½	teaspoon nutmeg
3	eggs
3	cups warm milk
½	cup sugar

Crumble bread and soak for 20 minutes in milk and salt. Combine eggs, sugar, vanilla and nutmeg; beat well. Pour mixture over bread; stir lightly. Steam tightly covered with foil in pan and set in hot water for about 45 minutes at 350 degrees. Cover with meringue and bake at 300 degrees 15 minutes. Serve with Brown Sugar Sauce.

Sauce:	½	pound brown sugar
	¼	cup flour
	1	cup boiling water
	¼	cup butter
	½	teaspoon vanilla

Mix sugar and flour well. Add boiling water. Cook mixture until thick. Remove from fire and add butter and vanilla.

Shaker Village at Pleasant Hill

"We make you kindly welcome" best describes this once utopian community that has made a lasting statement in the Bluegrass.

Harrodsburg, Kentucky
3501 Lexington Road ~ Harrodsburg, KY 40330 ~ 800-734-5611

Eagle Eyrie

Chocolate Éclair Dessert

27   whole graham crackers
3   cups cold milk (skim)
2   small packages Jello pudding mix (French Vanilla or
      Vanilla)
1   12 ounce Cool Whip, thawed
1   16 ounce container of Ready to Spread Chocolate
      Frosting

Arrange crackers in bottom of dish. Pour milk in bowl, add pudding mix. Beat with wire whisk 2 minutes. Gently stir in cool whip, mix good. Spread ½ pudding over crackers, place remaining crackers on top, then remaining pudding mix. Place another layer of crackers. Microwave frosting on HIGH for 30-45 seconds. Then spread over top layer of crackers. Refrigerate at least 4 hours or overnight.

Sherried Fruit Compote

1	12 ounce box pitted prunes
1	6 ounce package dried apricots
1	20 ounce can pineapple chunks, undrained
1	11 ounce can mandarin orange slices, undrained
1	21 ounce can cherry pie filling
½	cup cooking sherry

Place prunes and apricots in a 2 quart oblong baking dish. Combine remaining ingredients and pour over dried fruit. Bake at 350 degrees, uncovered, for one hour. Serve for breakfast, brunch, lunch or dinner. Serves 12

Eagle Eyrie
The Inn features four luxurious guest rooms completely furnished with antiques. Breakfast is served buffet style in the dining room.

Camilla, Georgia
135 East Broad Street ~ Camilla, GA 31730 ~ 229-336-8811

A True Inn

Pecan Pie Muffins

1	cup brown sugar
1	cup pecan pieces
½	cup all purpose flour
2	eggs, beaten
⅔	cup melted butter (not margarine)

Mix all dry ingredients and set aside. Mix butter and eggs. Add to dry ingredients. Pour into greased and floured mini-muffin tins. Bake at 350 degrees for 20-25 minutes.

Note: makes about 36 of the mini-muffin size, 16 of the medium muffin size and 8 of the large muffins. If you wish to make them like brownies in a 13 x 9, double the recipe.

A True Inn

Listed on the National register, the architecture is Greek Revival, and each room is named for a famous Lexingtonian.

Lexington, Kentucky

467 West Second St. ~ Lexington, KY 40507 ~ 859-252-6166

Von-Bryan Inn

Moist Java Cake

2	cups plain flour
2	cups sugar
¼	cup cocoa
2	teaspoons baking soda
1	teaspoon baking powder
2	eggs
1	cup hot brewed coffee
1	cup milk
1	teaspoon vanilla
½	cup butter, softened

Mix flour, sugar, cocoa, soda and baking powder. Add remaining ingredients. Pour into greased and floured 8 x 10-inch pan or two round 8-inch pans. Batter will be thin. Bake at 350 degrees for 25-30 minutes or until cake tests done.

Frosting:	3	cups powdered sugar
	3	tablespoons hot coffee
	3	tablespoons cocoa
	3	tablespoons butter, softened
	3	tablespoons Kahlua, or 1 teaspoon vanilla

Mix to spreading consistency adding small amounts of coffee or sugar as needed.

Von-Bryan Inn

This lovely mountaintop retreat has spectacular views at every turn.

Sevierville, Tennessee
2402 Hatcher Mountain Rd. ~ Sevierville, TN 37862 ~ 865-453-9832

South Central Region

South Central Region

Borgman's Bed & Breakfast

Divinity Candy

4	egg whites
4	cups sugar
1	cup water
1	cup white syrup
½	teaspoon cream of tartar
½	teaspoon vanilla

Beat egg whites until stiff, then add cream of tartar. In a separate bowl, mix sugar, water and syrup. Boil syrup mixture to 250 degrees. Slowly add half of the syrup to egg whites, beating continuously. Boil the rest of the syrup mixture to 280 degrees. Again beat egg white mixture as you slowly add the rest of the syrup. Add vanilla. Let set until cool. Beat occasionally, and it should lose its glossy look. Drop with spoon onto waxed paper.

Borgman's Bed & Breakfast
This old-fashioned inn is located in historic Arrow Rock, a bustling river town during the 1880s.

Arrow Rock, Missouri
706 Van Buren ~ Arrow Rock, MO 65320 ~ 660-837-3350

Chef Andre's Brandy Bread Pudding

2   loaves french bread (torn into 3-inch pieces) toasted
1   pound cake (strawberry glazed) torn into pieces
10 whole eggs
2   cans sweet condensed milk
3   cartons hazelnut creamer
3   tablespoons nutmeg
2   tablespoons cinnamon
1   pound melted butter
2   tablespoons almond extract

Toast french bread, add strawberry glazed pound cake, place in baking pan (17¼ x 11 ¾ x 2¼-inch). Mix remaining ingredients with a large whisk. Pour over bread and cake. Cover with foil and bake 1 hour 325 degrees. Uncover and bake 15 minutes at 350 degrees. Scoop out portions and pour hot brandy sauce over pudding. Top with chopped roasted nut and sprinkle with powdered sugar. Garnish with a strawberry.

Chef Andre's Brandy Sauce

10 egg yolks
2   cartons whipping cream
2   bags of powder sugar
2   cups of brandy
2   tablespoons of almond extract
1   pound of butter (melted)

Mix all ingredients well. Place sauce in a double boiler on medium heat and stir occasionally until bubbles and serve.

Cedar Grove Vicksburg
Listed on the national register, this is one of Vickburg's most elaborately restored grand luxe estates and it dates back to 1840.

Vicksburg, Mississippi
2200 Oakstreet ~ Vicksburg, MS 39180 ~ 800-862-1300

Clotted Cream Puffs with Rhubarb Sauce

Puffs: ½   cup butter
              1   cup unbleached flour
              ¼   teaspoon salt
              4   eggs

Melt butter in microwave. Pour into saucepan and turn on heat. Add flour and salt immediately; stir vigorously. Cook and stir until mixture forms balls that won't separate. Add eggs, one at a time, beating after each until smooth. Drop by heaping tablespoons, 3 inches apart, onto greased cookie sheet. Bake at 450 degrees for 15 minutes, then at 325 degrees for 25 minutes. Remove from oven and split. Put back into oven to dry; about 20 minutes.

Filling: 1   cup vanilla yogurt
              ¾   cup whipping cream (whipped)
              ½   cup lemon curd

Fold all ingredients together to create filling. Fill puffs. Top with lid.

Sauce: 1   package frozen Christmas Rhubarb
              3-6 drops of red food coloring
              ⅓   cup of Bed & Breakfast liqueur
              ½   cup of orange juice
              ¾   cup of sugar

Mix all ingredients. Cook on low heat; boiling to soften the rhubarb. Mash with potato masher until of thick consistency. Pour Christmas Rhubarb sauce over Clotted Cream Puff and serve.

The Empress of Little Rock

Listed on the National Register, this is a fine example of Victorian architecture and dates back to 1888.

Little Rock, Arkansas

2120 S. Louisiana St. ~ Little Rock, AR 72206 ~ 501-374-7966

The Grandison at Maney Park

Pumpkin Cookies

1	cup shortening
2	cups brown sugar
3	eggs
1¾	cups pumpkin
½	cup sour cream
3	cups flour
1	teaspoon baking powder
1	teaspoon soda
½	teaspoon salt
1½	teaspoon cinnamon
¼	teaspoon ginger
½	teaspoon nutmeg
1	cup raisins
1	cup nuts

Cream shortening and sugar. Add eggs and blend well. Sift dry ingredients. Add sour cream to pumpkin. Add dry ingredients to creamed mixture alternately with sour cream and pumpkin. Add raisins and nuts. Mix well. Drop by spoonfuls onto greased baking sheets. Bake at 350 degrees for 15-20 minutes. Makes 4 dozen. Can cool, package and freeze, if you desire.

Grape Ice Cream

Juice of 2 lemons (4 ounces)
1   cup sugar (2 cups, depending on taste)
1   pint grape juice (2 small cans frozen)
Milk

Dissolve lemon juice and sugar together. Add grape juice, do not dilute. Add enough milk to fill freezer.

The Grandison at Maney Park
This architectural beauty is an outstanding example of Victorian style. Conveniently located, the Grandison is lovely.

Oklahoma City, Oklahoma
1200 N. Shartel ~ Oklahoma City, OK 73103 ~ 405-232-8778

Huckleberry Inn

Huckleberry Jam Cake

1   cup butter
2   cups sugar
4   eggs
2   cups huckleberry jam
3   cups flour
2   teaspoons allspice
1   teaspoon baking soda
1   teaspoon baking powder
2   teaspoons cinnamon
1   cup buttermilk

Preheat oven to 300 degrees. Grease and flour 3 9-inch cake pans. Cream butter and sugar. Add well-beaten eggs. Add jam. Mix all dry ingredients together and add in small amounts alternately with the buttermilk, beating as you go. Bake at 300 degrees for 40 minutes. After cakes are cool they should be frosted with a sauce between each layer and raisins, pecans and walnuts should also be put between each layer.

Sauce: 1   cup of cream
            2   cups sugar
            1   tablespoon butter

Topping: 1   cup of raisins
            1½ cups of walnut halves
            1½ cups of pecan halves

Combine the cream and sugar in a heavy saucepan. Bring to a boil and then cook 2-3 minutes. Turn off fire and let cool a little and beat till it thickens a little. Add butter and spread between each layer and on top but just let it drip down sides. Cover the sauce between each layer with the topping arranged decoratively.

Huckleberry Inn
Brings back to life the spirit and feeling of those glorious days of the deep south.
Leesville, Louisiana
702 Alexandria Hwy ~ Leesville, LA 71446 ~ 318-238-4000

Lamothe House

Lamothe House Pecan Pralines

1½ cups white sugar
½   stick butter
1   teaspoon vanilla
½   cup chopped or whole pecans
½   cup brown sugar
½   cup evaporated milk
    pinch baking soda

Cook sugar and milk over medium heat, stirring until it starts to boil. Add butter, pecans, and soda. Cook, stirring occasionally until soft ball stage (238 degrees). Remove from fire and beat with spoon until creamy and mixture begins to thicken. Drop by teaspoonfuls on buttered flat surface or waxed paper. If mixture becomes too hard, return to heat and add a little water.

Lamothe House
Within walking distance to the French Market and historic Jackson Square, this inn provides a glimpse into the wealth of the early 19th century.

New Orleans, Louisiana
621 Esplanade Ave. ~ New Orleans, LA 70116 ~ 888-696-9575

Madewood Plantation

Bread Pudding with Whiskey Sauce

1	loaf french bread
3	eggs
1	quart milk
2	cups sugar
1	cup raisins
1	tablespoon vanilla
½	stick butter

Mix bread and milk. Add eggs, sugar, raisins, and vanilla. Melt butter and pour into baking dish. Bake at 350 degrees until set.

Sauce:

Melt one stick butter. Add sugar and cook until dissolved. Beat one egg and add a little sugar mixture to egg and return to saucepan. Add a little whiskey to taste.

Madewood Plantation
Built in 1846, this is an outstanding example of Greek Revival architecture.

Napoleonville, Louisiana
4250 Hwy 308 ~ Napoleonville, LA 70390 ~ 985-369-7151

Bread Pudding in Rum Sauce

2	loaves white bread, broken in pieces
6	eggs, beaten
1	teaspoon vanilla
2	cups milk
2	cups water, warmed
2	cups sugar
½	pound margarine, melted

Mix water and margarine in large bowl. Put broken bread into the mixture and stir. Add milk and stir. Add vanilla, eggs and sugar; stir well. Pour into a 12 x 16-inch baking pan and bake at 350 degrees for one hour.

Sauce:	½	stick butter
	¼	cup sugar
	16	ounces whipped topping
	2-3	ounces white rum (to taste)

Melt the butter, add sugar and mix together in a bowl until the sugar is dissolved. Add whipped topping and whip with a wire whip. Drizzle the rum into the mixture a little at a time.

Nottoway Plantation

Listed on the national register, this American castle is the ultimate in Southern grandeur and hospitality.

White Castle, Louisiana

30970 Hwy. 405, the Mississippi River Rd. ~ White Castle, LA 70788-3603~ 225-545-2730

Oak Alley

Plantation Pecan Pie

¾ cup raw sugar
1 tablespoon all purpose flour
1 pinch salt
3 eggs well beaten
1 cup light corn syrup
1 teaspoon vanilla extract
2 tablespoons softened butter
1½ tablespoons pecans, coarsely chopped
1 unbaked 9-inch pastry shell

Combine dry ingredients in large mixing bowl. Add eggs, syrup, vanilla and butter. Beat with electric mixer until blended. Stir in pecans. Pour mixture into pastry shell. Bake at 350 degrees for hour and 15 minutes or until knife inserted in middle comes out clean.

Oak Alley
This outstanding colonial mansion has even appeared in encyclopedias.
Vacherie, Louisiana
Great River Rd. ~ Rt. 2, Box 10 ~ Vacherie, LA 70090 ~ 504-265-2151

Salmen-Fritchie House

Bread Pudding with Whiskey Sauce

1	10 ounce loaf stale French bread, crumbled (or 6-8 cups any type bread)
4	cups milk
2	cups sugar
8	tablespoons butter, melted
3	eggs
2	tablespoons vanilla
2	cups raisins
1	cup coconut
1	cup chopped pecans
1	tablespoon cinnamon
1	tablespoon nutmeg

Combine all ingredients; mixture should be very moist but not soupy. Pour into buttered 9 x 12-inch or larger baking dish. Place into a non-preheated oven. Bake at 350 degrees for approximately one hour and 15 minutes, until top is golden brown. Serve warm with sauce.

Sauce: ½ cup butter (1 stick, ¼ pound)
1½ cup powdered sugar
2 egg yolks
½ cup bourbon (to taste)

Cream butter and sugar over medium heat until all butter is absorbed. Remove from heat and blend in egg yolk. Pour in bourbon gradually to taste, stirring constantly. Sauce will thicken as it cools. Serve warm over warm bread pudding. Makes 16-20 servings.
NOTE: For a variety of sauces, just substitute your favorite fruit juice or liqueur to complement your bread pudding.

Salmen-Fritchie House
This is a fine example of the grand old homes found in the deep south at the turn of the century and it has remained in the same family since 1895.

Slidell, Louisiana
127 Cleveland Ave. ~ Slidell, LA 70458 ~ 985-645-3600

Schmidt's Guest House

Spicy Apple Pudding

1	cup sugar
1	teaspoon cinnamon
½	teaspoon cloves
1	egg well beaten
1	cup flour
1	teaspoon soda
4	tablespoons melted shortening
3	large grated apples

Mix all ingredients together and bake in greased baking dish at 350 degrees for 45 minutes. Serve warm with whipped cream.

Schmidt's Guest House
A classic example of the simple, graceful architecture of the 18th and 19th centuries.

Hermann, Missouri
300 Market St. ~ Hermann, MO 65041 ~ 314-486-2146

Southwest Region

Southwest Region

Apple Blossom Inn

Cocoa Kisses

1	cup sugar
3	egg whites
⅛	teaspoon salt
2	teaspoons water
1	teaspoon vanilla
3	tablespoons cocoa
¾	cup chopped pecans

Preheat oven to 250 degrees. Sift sugar. Whip egg whites and salt until stiff but not dry. Gradually add half the sugar. Combine water and vanilla. Add the liquid a few drops at a time alternately with the remaining sugar, whipping constantly. Fold in cocoa and pecans. Drop the batter onto a lightly greased cookie sheet and shape into cones. Bake until kisses are firm to the touch, but soft inside. Remove from pan while hot. Makes 40 1-inch meringues.

Apple Blossom Inn
Built in 1879, is a fine example of Victorian Architecture.

Leadville, Colorado
120 West 4th St. ~ Leadville, CO 80461 ~ 800-982-9279

Arizona Biltmore

Poached Pears with Almond Raisin Stuffing and Raspberry Sauce

6   Bartlett pears, cored and peeled
5   ounces almond paste
1½ cups white wine
1   cup maple syrup
3   ounces raisins

Poach pears in liquid until pears are soft. Remove when finished and let cool. Mix almond paste with raisins and stuff pears.

Sauce: 1   cup poaching liquid
              2   cups red wine
              2   pints raspberry puree
                   lemon juice to taste

Puree raspberries and cool poaching liquid. Add red wine and lemon juice. Strain. If sauce is too tart, adjust with small amount of sugar. Arrange pears on glass plate and cover with sauce. Serves 6.

Arizona Biltmore
This architectural wonder has a history that's as colorful as the beautiful land-scaped grounds that surround it.

Phoenix, Arizona
2400 East Missouri ~ Phoenix, AZ 85016 ~ 602-955-6600

Creamy Berry Royal

1   pound sour cream
2½ cups heavy cream
1   cup sugar
1¼ teaspoon gelatin
1   teaspoon vanilla

Combine cream, sugar and gelatin in heavy sauce pan and heat (do not boil). Let cool, then add sour cream and vanilla. Mix until smooth, pour into glasses and let solidify in refrigerator for around 8 hours. Top with fruit of your choice.

Benbow Inn
This national registered landmark has welcomed visitors since 1926.

Garberville, California
445 Lake Benbow Dr. ~ Garberville, CA 95542 ~ 707-923-2124

Briar Rose Bed and Breakfast

Briar Rose Shortbread Cookies

2   cups butter
4   cups flour
1   cup confectioner's sugar
    pinch of salt

Cream butter and sugar together, add flour and salt. Shape into balls and press down with three fingers. Fill center with jam or nuts, if desired. Bake at 325 degrees for 20-25 minutes or until golden brown.

Briar Rose Bed and Breakfast
This Bed and Breakfast is English Country and furnished in antiques. Chocolates on the pillow.

Boulder, Colorado
2151 Arapahoe Ave. ~ Boulder, CO 80302 ~ 303-442-3007

Campbell Ranch Inn

Raspberry Cream Cheese Coffee Cake

Cake: 2½ cups flour
3/4 cup sugar
3/4 cup butter
½ teaspoon baking powder
½ teaspoon baking soda
¼ teaspoon salt
3/4 cup dairy sour cream
1 egg
1 teaspoon almond extract

Preheat oven to 350 degrees. In a large bowl, combine flour and sugar; cut in the butter using a pastry blender until mixture resembles coarse crumbs. Remove 1 cup of crumbs for topping. To remaining crumb mixture, add baking powder, baking soda, salt, sour cream, egg and almond extract. Blend well. Spread batter over bottom and 2 inches up sides of a greased and floured 9-inch springform pan. Batter should be ¼-inch thick on sides.

Continued on page 182

Southwest Region

Continued from page 181

Filling: 1   **8-ounce package cream cheese**
             ¼   **cup sugar**
             1   **egg**
             ½   **cup raspberry jam**

In small bowl, combine cream cheese, ¼ cup sugar and egg; blend well. Pour over batter in pan. Spoon jam evenly over the cheese filling.

Topping: ½   **cup sliced almonds (2-ounce package)**

In a small bowl, combine 1 cup of reserved crumbs and almonds; sprinkle over top. Bake at 350 degrees for 50-60 minutes or until cream cheese is set and crust is a deep golden brown. Cool 15 minutes, remove sides and cool completely.

Campbell Ranch Inn
This fine contemporary-style inn is surrounded by 35 rolling acres.
Geyserville, California
1475 Canyon Road ~ Geyserville, CA 95441

Dream Cheesecakes

Filling: 3   8-ounce packages softened cream cheese
              1½ teaspoons vanilla extract
              1   cup sugar
              5   eggs

Line 12 muffin tins with cupcake liners. Cream the cheese with vanilla. Add sugar and eggs and beat well. Spoon mixture into cupcake liners, filling about half full. Bake for 20 to 25 minutes or until tops crack slightly.

Topping: 1   pint dairy sour cream
              ¼   cup sugar
              1   teaspoon vanilla

Combine all ingredients and mix well. Spoon a small amount of topping onto each cake and bake for 5 minutes. Cool on racks and refrigerate until ready to serve. May be garnished with fresh strawberry, kiwi or pineapple before serving. Makes a nice light dessert after a heavy meal or for a ladies' luncheon.

Party Sponge Cake

2 cups flour
1½ cups sugar
7 egg yolks
3 teaspoons baking powder
½ cup cooking oil
1 teaspoon salt
½ cup cold water
7 egg whites
½ teaspoon cream of tartar

In large bowl, put first 7 ingredients and beat until smooth. Meanwhile, whip the egg whites and cream of tartar in small bowl until stiff peaks are formed. Gradually add to mixture in large bowl and fold gently only until blended. (This can be made in regular round cake pan or double batter and make in large oblong pan.)

Bake in 325 degree oven for 40 minutes. Increase to 360 degrees and bake 15 minutes longer until cake tests done. For birthday cakes, cut in half and brush cut halves with rum. Add cream and put cake back together. Frost as desired.

Cream: 1 pint milk
½ cup sugar
1 egg yolk
rind of one lemon
1 cup flour

Cook together in top of double boiler until thick and creamy. Remove lemon rinds and spread on cake half.

Pineapple Upside Down Cake

Base: 2   cups brown sugar
                ¼   cup butter
                     pineapple slices
                     cherries
                     walnuts (optional)

Melt butter and sugar in baking pan. Arrange pineapple slices and cherries, walnuts if desired.

Batter: 3   eggs
                1   cup sugar
                1   cup flour
                1   tablespoon boiling water
                2   teaspoons vinegar
              1½ teaspoons baking powder
                ¼   teaspoon salt

Separate eggs. Beat whites until stiff, add vinegar. Set aside. Beat egg yolks until thick and creamy; add sugar gradually and continue to mix until smooth. Add water, flour, salt and baking powder, and mix. Fold in egg whites with vinegar.
Add batter to cake pan and bake at 350 degrees for 45 minutes. Turn out carefully so that pineapple slices will stay on top.

Heritage Park
Located in historic Old Town San Diego, this is an elegant Victorian Inn.

San Diego, California
2470 Heritage Park Row ~ San Diego, CA 92110 ~ 619-299-6832

Historic Castle Marne

Lisa's Raspberry Cheesecake

1½ cups vanilla wafer crumbs
¼   cup butter, melted
1   envelope unflavored gelatin
¼   cup cold water
2   8-ounce packages cream cheese, softened
1   tablespoon lemon juice
1   teaspoon grated lemon peel
1   7-ounce jar marshmallow cream
3   cups Cool Whip
2   cups raspberries

Combine crumbs and butter and then press onto bottom of a 9-inch springform pan. Chill. In medium saucepan, soften gelatin in water. Stir over low heat until dissolved. Remove from heat and slowly add cream cheese and blend well. Add juice and peel. Beat in marshmallow cream. Fold in Cool Whip. Puree raspberries and fold into cream cheese mixture. Pour over crust. Chill until firm. Remove outside of springform pan. Garnish with whipped cream, lemon peel and fresh raspberries. Serves 10-12.

Ursula's Red Velvet Victorian Cake

Cake:
- ½ cup shortening
- 1½ cups sugar
- 2 eggs
- 1 teaspoon vanilla
- 2 tablespoons red food coloring
- 2 tablespoons water
- 2 cups cake flour
- 1 teaspoon salt
- 1 teaspoon soda
- 2 tablespoons cocoa
- 1 cup buttermilk
- 1 tablespoon vinegar

Preheat oven to 350 degrees. Grease and flour two 9-inch cake pans. In a large mixing bowl, cream together shortening and sugar. Add eggs, vanilla, red food coloring, and water and mix well. In a separate bowl, mix together flour, salt, soda and cocoa. In another bowl, mix together buttermilk and vinegar. Alternately add flour mixture and buttermilk mixture to the shortening mixture, stirring after each addition. Divide evenly between the two prepared pans. Bake for about 30 minute or until toothpick inserted in the center comes out clean. After cooling slightly, remove from the pans and cool completely on cooling racks.

Frosting:
- 8 ounces cream cheese
- ½ cup butter
- 1 pound powdered sugar
- 1 teaspoon vanilla
- Assorted fresh flowers

Cream together the cream cheese and butter. Add vanilla and mix well. Slowly add powdered sugar and mix until fluffy. If the mixture is too thick to spread, add a little cream or milk to make it a thinner consistency. Trim the top of one of the cakes to make if flat on the top. Frost the top of the trimmed cake. Place the other cake on top of the frosted cake. Frost the top and sides of the layered cakes. Decorate the cake with fresh flowers. Serves 16.

Southwest Region

Edie's Crème de Menthe Pie

18 large marshmallows
½ cup milk
3 tablespoons Crème de Menthe liqueur
¼ teaspoon peppermint extract
1 cup whipping cream, whipped
20 Double-Stuf Oreo cookies
⅛ cup semisweet chocolate chips

Melt marshmallows and milk in a large saucepan. Remove from heat and chill 30 minutes. Add Crème de Menthe and peppermint extract and whisk until smooth. Fold in whipped cream. Grind up Oreos until they form a paste. Spray an 8-inch pie pan. Pat Oreo mixture into bottom and sides of pie pan. Pour marshmallow mixture into the pie shell. Melt the chocolate chips and thin with a little oil. Drizzle over the pie. Chill thoroughly, slice and serve. Serves 6-8.

Diane's Fresh Fruit Trifle

6   cups angel food cake, cut in 1-inch cubes
3   medium peaches
3   tablespoons lemon juice
1   quart sliced strawberries
1½ cups seedless red or green grapes
1   cup kiwi
2   8-ounce cartons vanilla yogurt
1   carton sour cream
     Whipped cream
⅓   cup sherry

Mix sour cream and vanilla yogurt. Dip peach slices in lemon juice. Put layer of angel food cake on bottom of trifle dish and sprinkle with part of the sherry. Continue to layer fruit, sour cream mixture, cake, sherry and whipped cream. Decorate top with whipped cream and fruit.
You can use pound cake or ladyfingers in place of the angel food cake. You can substitute any flavored liqueur in place of the sherry. Any fruits can be used for variations in color. Pears, pineapple, blueberries, raspberries and bananas are all wonderful in this dessert!

Historic Castle Marne

This architectural beauty is one of Denver's greatest historic mansions. It has been featured on the National Public Television series, Inn Country, U.S.A. Afternoon tea. Gourmet candlelight six course dinners.

Denver, Colorado

1572 Race Street ~ Denver, CO 80206 ~ 303-331-0621

Chocolate Espresso Cheesecake

1½ cups chocolate wafer cookies crushed
2   tablespoons butter melted
1½ tablespoons instant coffee powder
3   teaspoons vanilla
48   ounces cream cheese softened
1   cup sugar
4   large eggs room temperature
1   cup sour cream
12   ounces semisweet chocolate melted

Line bottom of 10-inch springform pan with foil. Wrap extra sheet of foil all around outside of pan. Mix crumbs with melted butter and press cookie crumbs into bottom of pan. In a small cup, combine the espresso powder and vanilla and stir with a small rubber spatula until the powder is dissolved. In a large bowl beat the cream cheese at low speed until creamy. Beat in the sour cream. Gradually add in the sugar and beat at medium speed until well blended.

At low speed add the eggs one at a time, beating well after each addition. Beat in the espresso mixture. Beat in the melted chocolate. Pour mixture into prepared pan and smooth the top with spatula. Place the cheesecake in a roasting pan on the lower rack of the oven. Pour in enough boiling water into the roasting pan to come halfway up the side of the pan. Bake at 325 degrees for approximately 1½ hours or until the top is slightly puffed and the center is just firm. Turn off the oven, prop open the oven door (not very far) and allow the cheesecake to cool in the oven 1 hour. Remove cheesecake from the roasting pan and remove the outer sheet of foil. Set the cheesecake on a wire rack until completely cool. Cover the pan with aluminum foil and refrigerate for 4 to 6 hours, or overnight. Run a thin-bladed knife around the edge of the cheesecake to loosen it from the side of the pan. Remove the springform ring. Transfer it to a serving platter.

Topping: 3   ounces semisweet chocolate
3   tablespoons butter
2   teaspoons light corn syrup

Over low heat, heat 3 ounces semisweet chocolate, 3 tablespoons butter and 2 teaspoons of light corn syrup stirring frequently until melted and smooth. Remove from heat, stir until glaze cools and thickens slightly and pour over cheesecake. Makes 20 servings.

Southwest Region

Dutch Apple Pie

Crust: 1½   cups all-purpose flour
               1   teaspoon salt
               ½   cup shortening
               ¼   cup milk
               1   egg, beaten

In a bowl, mix flour and salt. Cut in shortening until smooth. Gradually add milk and egg; blend well. On a floured board, roll dough out, place in a 9-inch pie pan; set aside.

Filling: ¾   cup sugar
              2   tablespoons flour
                pinch salt
              1   egg, beaten
              ½   teaspoon vanilla
              1   cup sour cream
              2   cups apple, chopped
              1   teaspoon cinnamon
              ½   teaspoon nutmeg
              ¼   teaspoon ginger

In a mixing bowl, combine dry ingredients. Add egg, vanilla and sour cream; stir until smooth. Add apples, mix well. Pour into pie crust and bake at 375 degrees for 15 minutes. Reduce heat to 325 degrees for 30 minutes more.

Topping: ⅓   cup all-purpose flour
              ⅓   cup brown sugar
              2   tablespoons butter
              1   tablespoon cinnamon

Combine flour, sugar and cinnamon. Cut in butter until crumbly. Sprinkle topping over pie, bake an additional 20 minutes. Serve warm or chilled. Serves 8.

Historic Plaza Hotel
Historic Plaza Hotel has been a gathering place for locals and travelers since 1882.

Las Vegas, New Mexico
230 Plaza ~ Las Vegas, NM 87701-3433 ~ 800-328-1882

Sweet Memories   192

the lodge on the desert

Banana Chantilly

3   egg whites
¾   cup granulated sugar
½   teaspoon vanilla
½   teaspoon vinegar

Beat egg whites nearly stiff. Gradually add granulated sugar, beating constantly. Add vanilla and vinegar. Beat until well blended. Divide meringue into two parts and place each part, shaped to fit the tray of a refrigerator, on a buttered baking sheet. Bake at 275 degrees for 40-45 minutes or until delicately browned. Remove from oven and cool. Put together with the following:

1   cup banana pulp
1½ tablespoons lemon juice
¼   cup confectioners sugar
¼   teaspoon salt
1   cup heavy whipped cream

Combine banana pulp, salt and lemon juice. Add sugar to whipped cream and fold into banana mixture. Place one baked meringue in refrigerator tray. Cover with filling and add second meringue. Freeze for around 3 hours. Serves 6 to 8.

The Lodge on the Desert
Views are magnificent and delightful scents of fresh flowers are everywhere.

Tuscon Arizona
Box 42500 ~ Tucson, AZ 85733 ~ 602-325-3366

Southwest Region

The Pelican Inn

Sweet Cream Tart

9 ounces mincemeat
3 teaspoons almonds, finely chopped
12 ounces cream cheese, softened
¼ cup sugar
2 teaspoons lemon juice
   sweet pastry dough for 10-inch pan
1 egg
1 apple, peeled and sliced
2 egg yolks
1 teaspoon cinnamon
1 teaspoon sugar

Line pan with pastry dough. Spread mincemeat over dough and sprinkle evenly with almonds and apple. Beat cream cheese, adding sugar, then eggs, cinnamon, and lemon juice. Beat until smooth and creamy. Spoon mixture over apple. Bake at 400 degrees 20 minutes, lowering to 375 degrees and baking an additional 25 minutes. Sprinkle with remaining sugar. Serve at room temperature with whipped cream.

The Pelican Inn
Captures the spirit of 16th century England's west country.

Muir Beach, California
10 Pacific Way (Hwy. 1) ~ Muir Beach, CA 94965 ~ 415-383-6000

Preston House

White Chocolate Cheesecake

1	cup crushed chocolate wafers
½	cup walnuts (finely chopped)
4	tablespoons margarine (melted)
2	8-ounce packages cream cheese (softened)
½	cup sugar
½	teaspoon vanilla
2	eggs
8	ounces of white chocolate (melted)

Combine chocolate crumbs, nuts and margarine. Press into bottom of a 9-inch springform pan. Bake at 350 degrees for 10 minutes.

Combine cream cheese, sugar and vanilla in an electric mixer at medium speed. Mix until well blended. Add eggs one at a time, mixing well after each one. Blend in white chocolate, mix well. Pour over crust, bake at 350 degrees for 45 minutes. Loosen cake from rim of pan. Let cake cool completely before removing from pan. Garnish with strawberries or shaved milk chocolate or both. Enjoy!

Rugelach

1   cup margarine, softened
1   8-ounce package cream cheese, softened
2½ cups all purpose flour
¼   teaspoon salt
¾   cup sugar
1   cup raisins
1   cup walnuts (finely chopped)
1   tablespoon cinnamon
½   cup raspberry jelly

With electric mixer at medium speed beat margarine and cream cheese until well blended. Gradually add flour and salt. Form dough into a ball. Wrap in plastic wrap and refrigerate for 1 hour.

Combine sugar, raisins, walnuts and cinnamon in a small bowl. Divide dough into 5 equal pieces; shape into balls. On floured board roll 1 ball into a 9-inch circle. Spread lightly with jelly. Sprinkle ½ cup sugar mixture evenly over circle. Cut circle into 10 wedges. Starting at wide end, roll up each wedge, pinching end to seal.

Place rugelach on lightly greased baking sheet, cookie sheet. Repeat with remaining dough, jelly and sugar mixture. Bake 15 to 20 minutes in a 375 degree oven until rugelach are lightly browned. Cool on wire racks.

Preston House

This Queen Anne-style inn is filled with antiques in addition to a delightful garden house.

Santa Fe, New Mexico

106 E Faithway St. ~ Santa Fe, NM 87501-2213 ~ 505-982-3465

Washington School Inn

Ginger Snaps

¾ cup shortening
½ cup white sugar
½ cup brown sugar
¼ cup molasses
1 egg
2 cups flour
1 teaspoon soda
1 teaspoon cinnamon
½ teaspoon cloves
½ teaspoon ginger
½ teaspoon salt

Cream shortening and sugar. Add molasses and egg. Add dry ingredients. Chill for one hour. Roll into small balls and roll in sugar. Bake 9 minutes at 375 degrees.

Washington School Inn
This National Register landmark is superbly located to all outdoor activities.

Park City, Utah
543 Park Ave. ~ Park City, UT 84060 ~ 435-649-3800

Zion Overlook
Old-Fashioned Pineapple Upside-Down Cake

¾	cup brown sugar
½	cup butter
½	cup pecans or walnut halves or pieces
½	teaspoon cinnamon
1	can pineapple (8 slices)

Heat butter, sugar and cinnamon in bottom of heavy 10-inch skillet (2½-inches deep) until sugar is melted. Center one pineapple ring slice on sugar and place others around, filling the hollows with nuts.

Filling:	2	cups flour
	1	cup sugar
	1	cup milk
	½	cup butter
	2	eggs
	1	teaspoon vanilla
	½	teaspoon salt

Beat butter, add sugar and cream until light, then beat in eggs, one at a time. Measure flour, baking powder and salt, stir to mix. Add to butter mixture alternately with milk, beginning and ending with flour. Stir in vanilla, then pour over prepared topping in skillet. Cover with domed lid and bake over low heat until top springs back when touched, about 50-60 minutes. Release sides of cake and place a flat serving plate over top, then invert cake.

Zion Overlook
An unusual working ranch that sits on a 6,000 foot mesa overlooking Zion National Park.

La Verkin, Utah

Northwest Region

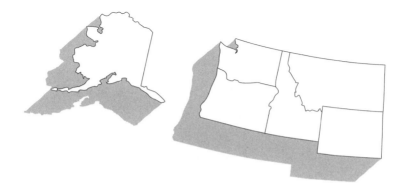

Northwest Region

A. Drummond's Ranch

Strawberry Glaze Pie

1	quart strawberries
¾	cup water
2	tablespoons cornstarch
¾	cup sugar
¼	teaspoon salt
1	baked 9-inch pie shell
	whipped cream

Crush 1 cup of the berries. Add water and bring to a boil. Simmer 3 minutes and add water if necessary to make 1 cup of liquid. Combine cornstarch, sugar and salt; add to liquid. Stir until smooth. Bring to a boil stirring constantly until liquid thickens. Cool. Place remaining berries in pie shell, and pour glaze over top. Cool in refrigerator and serve with whipped cream or vanilla ice cream.

Rhubarb Crunch

1   cup uncooked quick oats
½   cup flour
1   cup packed brown sugar
½   cup butter
3   cups diced rhubarb
1   tablespoon flour
½   cup sugar
1   teaspoon cinnamon
⅛   teaspoon salt
1   tablespoon water

Mix oats, flour, sugar, and butter until crumbly and put half of mixture in greased pan. Mix together rhubarb, flour, sugar, cinnamon, salt and water. Spread in pan, and top with remaining oat mixture. Bake in oven preheated to 350 degrees for 45 minutes. Serve hot! This is wonderful with ice cream.

Puff Pastry for Profiteroles

⅓   cup butter
1   cup water
⅛   teaspoon salt
1½   cup flour
4   medium eggs room temperature

In a saucepan, heat water, butter and salt over medium high heat till it boils and butter melts. Remove from heat and immediately dump all flour in and stir quickly forming a ball. Place pastry ball in mixing bowl and cool for 5 minutes. Beat in eggs at medium high speed ONE AT A TIME, beating well after each addition. Preheat oven to 375 degrees. Grease cookie sheet and drop pastry by teaspoon. Bake for 10 minutes, then reduce temperature to 350 and bake another 25 minutes, till they are golden. Cool on a rack, slit open and fill with ice cream or pudding, drizzle with hot fudge sauce!

Hot Fudge Sauce

1 ounce unsweet chocolate
¼ cup butter
¾ cup sugar
¼ cup cocoa powder
4-5 ounces evaporated milk
1 teaspoon vanilla
   dash of salt

Melt chocolate and butter in saucepan. Add sugar and cocoa, and stir until mixed. Gradually stir in milk; bring to just below a boil, remove from heat and add vanilla and dash of salt. For thicker sauce, use a bit less milk.

A. Drummond's Ranch
Offers fine accommodations just minutes from Cheyenne or Laramie.

Cheyenne/Laramie, Wyoming
399 Happy Jack Rd. ~ Cheyenne, Laramie, WY 82007 ~ 307-634-6042

Northwest Region

The Captain Whidbey Inn

Captain Whidbey Trifle

1   layer of white sponge cake (see Joy of Cooking or
    other standard reference cookbook)½-inch thick
    Raspberry jam*
    Vanilla pudding
    Sour cream
    Chopped almonds
      *Fresh raspberries work very well and are not as sweet as
      most jams or preserves.

Soak sponge cake with cocktail sherry. Put very thin layer of raspberry
jam on cake, cover with very thin layer of vanilla pudding, and very thin
layer of sour cream. Sprinkle chopped almonds lightly and repeat layers.
Make layers as thin as you can!

Captain Whidbey Washington Apple Cake

3	eggs
2	cups sugar
1	teaspoon vanilla flavoring
2	cups flour
2	teaspoons cinnamon
1	teaspoon baking soda
½	teaspoon salt
1	cup vegetable oil
1	cup chopped walnuts
4	cups thinly sliced, pared, tart apples

Beat eggs with mixer until thick and light, combining sugar and oil. Pour in eggs with mixer on medium speed. Stir flour, cinnamon, soda, and salt together; add to egg mixture. Add vanilla. Beat until thoroughly mixed. Stir in walnuts, spread apples in buttered 9 x 13-inch pan. Pour mixture over apples, spreading the batter to cover apples. Bake at 350 degrees for 1 hour. Cool, spread with cream cheese icing.

Icing:		
	2	3-ounce packages cream cheese
	¼	cup melted butter
	2	cups powdered sugar
	1	teaspoon lemon juice

Soften cream cheese. Beat until fluffy. Beat in melted butter, adding powdered sugar and lemon juice. Spread over Apple Cake and refrigerate until served.

The Captain Whidbey Inn

The Captain Whidbey Inn enjoys one of the northwest's most beautiful areas between Seattle and Vancouver.

Coupeville, Washington

2072 W Captain Whidbey Inn Rd. ~ Coupeville, WA 98239 ~ 360-678-4097

Northwest Region

Lone Mountain Ranch

Chocolate Kahlua Cashew Pie

1	cup sugar
1	cup light corn syrup
½	cup butter
1	cup chocolate chips
4	eggs, beaten
¼	cup Kahlua
1	teaspoon vanilla
¼	teaspoon salt
1	cup cashews
1	9-inch pie shell

Combine first three ingredients in a sauce pan until boiling. Pour into a stainless steel bowl. Add chocolate chips, stirring until melted. Allow to cool. Once cooled, add eggs and remaining ingredients. Pour into pie shell and bake for about an hour at 350 degrees.
Note: Pecans may be substituted for cashews.

Margarita Cheesecake

2	pounds cream cheese, room temperature
1½	cups sugar
⅓	cup lime juice
¼	cups tequila
¼	cups Grand Marnier
3	eggs

Cream the cream cheese and sugar together until they are the consistency of cake batter. Add liquids. Last, add eggs, one at a time, scraping the bowl between each addition. Bake in a water bath at 300 degrees for 40 minutes to 1½ hours, depending on elevation. Allow to cool at room temperature before refrigerating and topping. A sour cream topping goes well.

Lone Mountain Ranch

Big Sky, Montana
750 Lone Mountain Ranch Rd. ~ Box 160069 ~ Big Sky, MT 59716 ~ 800-514-4644

Alaskan Rhubarb Pie

2-3 cups fresh rhubarb (the brighter the color, the better)
1   cup dugar
¼   cup brown sugar
2   tablespoons lemon juice
3   tablespoons flour
2   teaspoons cinnamon

Cut up the fresh rhubarb, add sugars, lemon juice, flour and cinnamon; mix well to coat. Prepare your favorite pie crust; roll out the pie dough and fit into a 10-inch pie pan, add the rhubarb mixture and add your top crust. Seal the edges of pie crust by basting the edge of the bottom crust with water, add top crust and flute the edges nicely. You can baste the top crust with milk and sprinkle with a little sugar if you like. Bake at 425 degrees for 30 minutes, then turn the oven down to 350 degrees for another 45 minutes.

You can easily make this into a rhubarb custard pie by adding 2 beaten eggs to the original mixture. The eggs create a nice custard texture and flavor. You can substitute Egg Beaters, if you prefer.

Whaler's Cove Lodge
This world class resort offers your choice of superb saltwater and freshwater angling, and is located on a beautiful secluded beach overlooking Killianoo Harbor.

Angoon, Alaska
P.O. Box 101 ~ Angoon, AK 99820-0101 ~ 907-788-3123

Flourless Nut Torte

5	ounces semi-sweet chocolate (melted)
3	cups ground nuts
¾	cups sugar
5	ounces softened butter
4	eggs
	flavoring to taste (vanilla, almond, Grand Marnier, etc.)

Finely grind nuts with ¼-cup of sugar in food processor. Place in a large mixing bowl and set aside. Place soft butter, cream and remainder of sugar in food processor. Slowly add eggs, chocolate and flavoring. Blend and pour in ground nut mixture and fold together. Pour into a greased and floured spring form pan and bake at 325 degrees for one hour. Cool and remove from pan, inverted.

Topping: 7½ ounces semisweet chocolate
            1¾ cup butter

Place chocolate and butter into double boiler and heat until melted. Top torte and spread evenly.

Sweet Potato Pie

4-5 medium sized sweet potatoes (baked and pureed)
½ cup brown sugar
8 eggs
1 cup milk
1 can evaporated milk
½ cup white sugar
1½ teaspoons cinnamon
½ teaspoon nutmeg
¼ teaspoon cloves
¼ teaspoon allspice

Blend all ingredients together well and place in an unbaked deep dish pie shell and bake at 350 degrees for 45-60 minutes. Cool and serve with lightly sweetened whipped cream, topped with a sprinkle of cinnamon.

Chocolate Angel Food Cake

2 cups sugar
1¾ cups egg whites
½ cup cake flour
2 tablespoons cold water
1 teaspoon cream of tartar
½ teaspoon baking soda
½ teaspoon salt

Place water, egg whites, salt and cream of tartar in mixing bowl and whip at high speed until it forms peaks. Set aside. Mix sugar, flour and baking soda together and sift four times. Fold gently into egg white mixture and place in tube pan. Bake at 350 degrees for approximately 40 minutes. Invert and cool. Remove from pan and cut horizontally into three rings

Filling: 8 ounces semisweet chocolate
6 egg yolks
½ cup sugar
1 cup whipped heavy cream
3 tablespoons water

Heat together in a double boiler until melted and smooth. Remove from heat and beat in egg yolks. Let cool, then fold in heavy cream. Frost the top of each cake ring and restack. Cut into 12 and serve with grated white chocolate.

Averill's Flathead Lake Lodge
This truly family vacation captures the Old West.

Big Fork, Montana
P.O. Box 248 ~ Bigfort, MT 59911 ~ 406-837-4391

Havenshire Bed and Breakfast

Mother Ritchie's Lemon Pie 1916

1½   cups sugar
6   tablespoons corn starch (7 to hold shape)
1½   cups boiling water
1½   tablespoons grated rind
3   medium egg yolks
3   tablespoons butter
4   tablespoons fresh lemon juice

Mix sugar and corn starch in top of double boiler. Blend in boiling water. Cook over direct heat (stirring constantly) until thick. Set over boiling water and cook 10 minutes (stirring constantly). Beat egg yolks slightly, blend into hot mixture. Add butter, lemon juice and rind. Cool and pour into baked pie shell.

Blend 1 tablespoon cornstarch in 6 tablespoons sugar add to ½ water. Cook over direct heat until thick (stir constantly). Allow to cool add to unbeaten egg whites. Beat until stiff and holds shape. Put on pie (attach to edge of crust. Bake at 350 degrees for 12-18 minutes till golden brown. According to your oven.

Deluxe Pecan Pie

1   cup Karo
2   eggs, beaten
1   cup sugar
⅛   teaspoon salt
1   teaspoon vanilla
1   pecan meats

Line 8-inch pie pan with pastry. Mix beaten eggs, Karo, sugar, salt and vanilla and add 2 tablespoons of melted butter, then pecans.
Bake at 400 degrees for 40 minutes, depending on your oven.

Havenshire Bed and Breakfast
Located four miles from Interstate 5, this handsome Tudor-style inn provides good food and comfortable lodging to weary travelers.

Azalea, Oregon
1098 Hogum Creek Rd. ~ Azalea, OR 97410 ~ 541-837-3511

THE ◖◗ HEATHMAN HOTEL

Chocolate Gourmandise

Cake: 4   ounces butter
4   ounces dark bittersweet chocolate
3   eggs
1½ ounces cocoa
4½ ounces sugar

Chop the chocolate into bite-sized pieces and place into a bowl with the butter and melt gently over a double boiler. Stir occasionally. Place the eggs into a metal bowl and beat with an electric mixer or hand-whip until they are lemon colored, fluffy and leave a ribbon. Sift cocoa powder and sugar together. Add to the whipped eggs and mix well. Add well-mixed butter/chocolate mixture to the egg/cocoa mixture and mix for a few seconds on high speed. You will see the mixture thicken slightly. Butter eight 2 x 2-inch ramekins and pour mixture in, leaving ¼-inch to ⅓-inch space at the top (cake will inflate slightly during cooking). Bake in a water bath in a 275 degree oven for about 30-40 minutes. Turn upside down immediately onto wax or parchment paper and let sit for 1-2 minutes before checking for doneness. Otherwise, let sit 10-15 minutes before removing ramekin.

Leaf:
- 1 cup powdered sugar
- 4 ounces butter
- ¼ cup honey
- ½ cup egg whites
- 50 grams cocoa
- 90 grams flour

Cream sugar and butter until smooth, white and fluffy. Add honey to butter/sugar and whip. Add egg white very slowly, allowing whites to be thoroughly incorporated and emulsified before adding more. Sift cocoa and flour together and add to creamed mixture. Let rest overnight before using. Bake in a 235 degree oven for 4-7 minutes.

Sauce:
- 10 ounces bittersweet chocolate, chopped
- ½ cup milk (use more to thin)
- ½ teaspoon vanilla extract

Combine the chocolate milk in a bowl and melt gently over a hot water bath. Stir until smooth. Stir in vanilla, and a little more milk if sauce is too thick or looks curdled. Use warm or rewarm when needed. Can be prepared and kept refrigerated up to one week in advance.
Serve cake with chocolate sauce.

The Heathman Hotel
Open since 1927, this national landmark has 120 guest rooms.

Portland, Oregon
1001 SW Broadway at Salmon ~ Portland, OR 97205 ~ 503-241-4100

Huckleberry Pie

1   9-inch baked pastry shell
4   cups washed huckleberries
¾   cup water
3   tablespoons cornstarch
1   cup sugar
    lemon juice
    whipped cream or ice cream

Simmer one cup berries with water for 3-4 minutes. Combine cornstarch and sugar and add to cooking fruit. Simmer slowly until syrup is thick and a clear ruby red. When thickened, add lemon according to taste and cool slightly. Line pastry shell with 3 cups berries, pour the slightly cooled glaze over the raw berries. Mix gently with a fork to coat the fresh berries. Chill thoroughly. Serve with whipped cream or ice cream. Serves six to eight.

Huckleberry Daiquiri

¼   ounce white rum
¼   cup huckleberries
1   tablespoon simple syrup (½ water, ½ sugar)
1½ cups ice
¼   cup orange juice

Blend all ingredients in blender until smooth. Serve in tall glass and garnish with orange slice and cherry if desired. Serves one.

Hill's Resort
Located in the majestic wilderness of Idaho, this resort is sensational in all seasons.

Priest Lake, Idaho
4777 West Lakeshore Rd. ~ Priest Lake, ID 83856 ~ 208-443-2551

Creamy Banana Tiramisu

1½ cups milk
2   tablespoons instant coffee crystals
1   8-ounce package cream cheese, softened
¼   cup sugar
1   package (four ½-cup servings) instant vanilla pudding
     and pie filling
2   cups frozen non-dairy whipped topping, thawed
3   medium, ripe bananas
12   ladyfingers
¼   cup semi-sweet mini chocolate chips
     additional whipped topping for garnish

Stir together milk and coffee crystals until coffee is almost dissolved.
With hand mixer, beat together cream cheese and sugar in large bowl
until smooth and blended. Add pudding mix; gradually beat in coffee
mixture until smooth. Gently stir in whipped topping.
To assemble, place one ladyfinger in each four ounce cup. Top with
pudding mixture. Just before serving, place 4-5 banana slices on top of
pudding mixture. Top with whipped cream and garnish with a sprinkling
of mini chocolate chips. Serves 12.

Norwegian Fruit Pizza

Crust: ¾   cup butter
            ½   cup confectioner's sugar
            1½ cups all-purpose flour

Mix together butter, confectioner's sugar and flour until crumb-like. Do not melt butter. Pat into 15-inch pizza pan and bake at 350 degrees for 13-15 minutes until golden brown. Do not overbake.

Filling: 8   ounces cream cheese, softened
             ½   cup sugar
             2   cups fresh fruit, sliced (peaches, kiwi, berries, bananas, etc.)

With hand mixer, mix cream cheese, sugar and vanilla until smooth. Spread over cooled crust. Place fruit on top, so design will remain when cut into 12 wedges.

Glaze: 1   cup apple juice
            2   tablespoons cornstarch
            1   tablespoon lemon juice
            ½   cup sugar

Mix apple juice, cornstarch, lemon juice and sugar together in saucepan. Cook over medium heat until clear and thick, stirring constantly. Cool. Spread over pizza after slicing. Serves 12.

7 Gables Inn & Suites
A handsome Tudor-style structure near the Chena River.

Fairbanks, Alaska
4312 Birch Lane ~ Fairbanks, AK 99709 ~ 907-479-0751

Shoshone Lodge

Old Fashioned Bread Pudding

1   cup sugar
1   teaspoon cinnamon or nutmeg
1   cup raisins
4   cups milk scalded with ½ cup margarine
6   cups soft bread crumbs (8 cups for firmer pudding)
4   eggs slightly beaten
½   teaspoon salt
2   teaspoons vanilla

Heat oven to 350 degrees. Place bread crumbs in 3-quart baking dish. Blend in remaining ingredients. Place dish in pan of hot water 1-inch deep. Bake 40-45 minutes or until knife inserted 1 inch from edge comes out clean. Serve warm with orange sauce.

Sauce:

1	cup sugar
2	tablespoons cornstarch
2	cups boiling orange juice
4	tablespoons butter
3	tablespoons lemon juice
	few grains nutmeg
	few grains salt

Mix sugar and cornstarch. Add juice gradually, stirring constantly. Cover and boil 5 minutes, stirring occasionally. Remove from heat and add other ingredients. Makes 2 cups.

Shoshone Lodge
This rustic resort is truly an exciting place for the outdoorsman.

Cody, Wyoming
349 Yellowstone Hwy. ~ Cody, WY 82414 ~ 307-587-4044

Ginger Sorbet

1½   cups sugar
2   tablespoons minced ginger root
2   teaspoons grated lemon zest
4   cups water
2   cups nonfat vanilla yogurt

Combine sugar, ginger and lemon zest in a food processor bowl. Blend until ginger and zest are very fine. In a heavy saucepan the ginger mixture with 4 cups of water (using a cup or so of the water to flush all the flavorful mixture from the bowl). Boil, uncovered over medium heat for 10 minutes. Cool, blend in the vanilla yogurt. Freeze the mixture in an ice cream maker, following manufacturer's directions.
This sorbet has a rich flavor with a creamy texture and when served stays frozen longer than sorbets that have only a water base.

Steamboat Inn
Surrounded by a wilderness of Douglas firs and varieties of North Umpqua, this is truly a paradise for the outdoorsman.

Steamboat, Oregon
42705 North Umpaqua Hwy. ~ Steamboat, OR 97447 ~ 541-498-2230

Chocolate Raspberry Cake

6	ounces pastry flour
2	ounces cocoa butter
½	cup hot coffee
2	ounces butter
2	tablespoons apricot jam
1	pound semi-sweet Belgian chocolate
1	cup almonds, toasted and ground with berries (for garnish)
2	pints fresh raspberries
8	eggs
⅓	pound sugar
1	cup cream
2½	ounces melted butter

Sift together flour and cocoa. Whisk eggs with sugar over hot water until thick and has reached a temperature of 100 degrees. Remove from heat and whisk until cool. Mixture should be light and thick. Carefully fold in flour and cocoa mixture, adding butter. Bake in two well-greased 9 x 12-inch cake pans about 40 minutes. Tops should spring back when pressed.

Continued on page 224

Continued from page 223

Turn cakes out and, when cold, slice off top third. Carefully scoop out insides to make container with sides and bottom 2-inch thick. Melt jam and mix with berries. Fill cake with raspberries and jam. Return top slice and chill. Melt chocolate, coffee and butter together. In another pan, bring cream to a boil. Whisk together until completely combined. When chocolate has cooled, spread on top and sides of cake. Mask sides with almonds and top with a few berries. Serves 10-12.

The Winchester Inn

This handsome inn is furnished with period antiques. Evening meals are served overlooking tiered gardens.

Ashland, Oregon
35 South Second St. ~ Ashland, OR 97520 ~ 541-488-1113

North Central Region

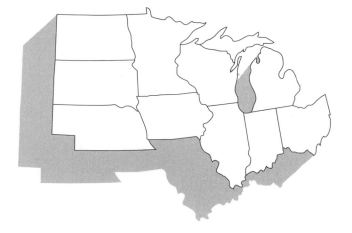

North Central Region

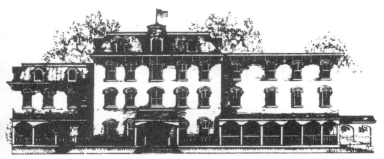

The Archer House

Galatoboureko
(Greek Custard Dessert with Lemon Syrup)

3	cups milk
½	cup sugar
1	tablespoon vanilla
¾	cup melted butter
½	cup plus 1 tablespoon quick cooking farina
3	cups heavy cream
7	egg yolks
½	pound phyllo leaves

Preheat oven to 375 degrees and grease a 9 x 13 x 3-inch baking pan. Combine milk and cream in a 3-quart saucepan, heating just to a boiling point on medium high, stirring occasionally to prevent scorching. While milk and cream are heating, combine sugar and farina in small bowl. In large mixing bowl beat egg yolks and vanilla well. When milk and cream come to boil, reduce heat to medium low and slowly sprinkle sugar/farina mixture into saucepan, stirring constantly 5-10 minutes until mixture is slightly thickened. Remove from heat and pour into egg yolks stirring until mixed. Lay one phyllo leaf into greased baking pan, allowing extra dough to slope up the sides of the pan, carefully brushing with melted butter. Repeat procedure for 5 more layers of phyllo. Pour custard mixture into pan and with sharp knife trim remaining phyllo to fit 9 x 13-inch pan exactly. Place a layer of dough on custard mixture, brushing with melted butter, repeating until 5 more layers are added. Cut top layer of dough only into 2-inch squares. Do not cut bottom. Bake 35 minutes.

Continued on page 228

North Central Region

Continued from page 227

Syrup: ¾   **cup sugar**
⅓   **cup water**
¼   **teaspoon finely grated lemon peel**
1   **tablespoon lemon juice**

Combine sugar and water in saucepan and heat until boiling. Reduce heat and simmer 8-10 minutes until thickened slightly. Remove from heat and add lemon juice and lemon peel.

While custard is still hot, pour lemon syrup over top of baking pan. Cool on rack for at least 1 hour before cutting. May be served warm or cold.

The Archer House

It was described as a grand event when it opened its doors, and today over a hundred years later, the greeting, "Welcome Friends" still stands.

Northfield, Minnesota
212 Division St. ~ Northfield, MN 55057 ~ 507-645-5661

Botsford Inn

Raspberry Gem Tarts

¼ cup unblanched almonds
½ cup fine, dry bread crumbs
¼ cup flour
½ teaspoon baking powder
¼ teaspoon salt
½ cup butter
¾ cup sugar
2 eggs
½ teaspoon vanilla extract
¼ teaspoon almond extract
  raspberry jam

Combine finely chopped almonds, bread crumbs, flour, baking powder and salt. Cream together butter, sugar, and eggs, and mix in vanilla and almond extracts. Add dry ingredients a little at a time, combining lightly but thoroughly. Line tart pans with thinly rolled pie crust, spooning a small amount of good raspberry jam into each, being certain to cover the bottom of each tart completely. Spoon batter over jam and bake 20-25 minutes or until golden brown at 375 degrees. Yields approximately 2 dozen tarts.

Botsford Inn

Once owned by Henry Ford, it entertained many famous visitors, including Thomas A. Edison.

Farmington Hills, Michigan
28000 Grand River Ave. ~ Farmington Hills, MI 48336-5919

North Central Region

The Golden Lamb

Osgood Pie

1   cup raisins cooked until plump
1   cup apples, peeled, cored, and chopped
1   cup pecans or other nuts, chopped
1   cup margarine, melted
4   eggs, beaten
1   tablespoon vinegar
2   cups sugar
    pastry for two single crust pies

Combine the first seven ingredients in a large bowl and mix well. Pour half of the mixture into each pie shell. Bake at 375 degrees for 40 minutes. Cool well before serving.

Ohio Shaker Lemon Pie

2   lemons
2   cups sugar
5   eggs
     pastry for a 2-crust 9-inch pie

Slice lemon rinds as thin as paper. Place them in a bowl and cover with sugar. Let stand for 2 hours or more. After lemons have mixed with sugar pour beaten eggs over the top. Fill unbaked pie crust with this mixture and cover with top crust. Cut small vents in top crust to let steam escape. Place in preheated 450 degree oven for 15 minutes, then lower temperature to 350 degrees and bake for an additional 30 minutes or until knife inserted comes out clean.

The Golden Lamb

This is Ohio's oldest continuous business. In the early days, travelers and coachmen unable to read, were told to look for "the sign of the golden lamb and stop for the night."

Lebanon, Ohio

27 S. Broadway ~ Lebanon, OH 45036 ~ 513-932-5065

Grand Hotel

Bamboo Peach

1¼ pound canned peaches
13 ounces bamboo shoots

Sauce:
1 cup sour cream
1 teaspoon cinnamon
½ teaspoon curry
¼ cup sugar
1 teaspoon mace
1 teaspoon nutmeg

In stainless steel bowl, mix peaches and shoots together. Mix ingredients for sauce by hand until smooth. Combine with the peaches and bamboo shoots. Serve in champagne glass or other suitable glassware. Serves 4.

Grand Hotel
This world's largest summer hotel has dominated the island of Mackinac since 1887.

Mackinac Island, Michigan
Mackinac Island, MI 49757 ~ 1-800-33-GRAND

Black Hills Hideaway

Black Hills Hideaway Apple Strudel

1	stick margarine, softened
1	stick butter, softened
2	cups all-purpose flour, sifted
2	tablespoons white vinegar
2	tablespoons water
3	egg yolks
6-8	cups apples, tart to semi-tart, pared and sliced
½	cup finely chopped nuts*
2-3	tablespoons cinnamon
½	cup sugar

Preheat oven to 350 degrees. Mix margarine, butter, flour, vinegar, watter and egg yolks, then refrigerate. Make the filling by combining apples, nuts, cinnamon and sugar. Dough should be split into two balls. Roll each ball into a rectangle and spread with half the filling. Roll up jelly-roll style. Bake on a lightly-greased cookie sheet for 20 minutes or until brown. Makes two strudels.
* For variety, ½ cup raisins can be added.

Black Hills Hideaway

Our eight guest rooms are tucked into a mountain chalet-style home with cathedral ceilings and a natural wood interior. Our home is located in the heart of the northern Black Hills on what was once a wagon trail in the late 19th century.

Deadwood, South Dakota
11744 Hideaway Rd. ~ Deadwood, SD 57732 ~ 605-578-3054

North Central Region

White Chocolate Mousse with Antlers

½ pound real white chocolate
(with cocoa butter content)
1 cup sugar
3 cups whipping cream
6 eggs, separated
white cream de cocoa

Melt chocolate in double boiler. In saucepan, heat egg whites and sugar over low heat, stirring until sugar has melted. Transfer to mixing bowl. Whip egg whites until stiff. Whip chilled cream until it is almost stiff (soft peaks). Beat egg yolks slightly. Add crème do cocoa. Blend well. Transfer melted chocolate to large bowl. Add egg yolk mixture. Blend. Add ⅓ of whipped egg whites. Blend well. Fold whipped cream into remaining whipped egg whites. Add chocolate mixture to cream and egg whites, folding carefully until well blended. Spoon into serving dishes and chill, or chill in mixing bowl and then using an ice cream scoop, serve in a cookie shell. For something extra special, the cookie shell could be coated with melted semisweet chocolate before placing the mousse in the shell. Top with Melba sauce. Makes about 10 servings.

Antler recipe continued on page 235

Chocolate Antlers
For White Chocolate Mousse
Previous page

6   ounces semisweet chocolate, cut in small pieces
1   tablespoon vegetable shortening

Tempered chocolate produces a beautiful satin sheen on the antlers. Place chocolate and shortening in top of double boiler over medium heat. Stir until chocolate is melted and is blended with the shortening. Remove from heat. Cook until chocolate starts to thicken. Line a baking sheet with parchment paper. Using a pastry bag with a writing tube, pipe chocolate onto parchment in the shape of antlers. Cool completely. Remove from parchment. To serve, insert antler into center of each serving of White Chocolate Mousse.

Marinade (Variation)

Cups: 6   ounces semisweet chocolate, cut in small pieces
1   tablespoon vegetable shortening

Cool chocolate mixture until it is cool enough to handle. Fan out cupcake liner, place a tablespoon of chocolate in the center of the liner. Use a small spatula or back of a spoon to spread the chocolate evenly inside the liner. Place the chocolate cup in a muffin tin. Repeat the procedure with the remaining liners. Refrigerate until chocolate is hardened. Carefully remove foil liners before serving. The cups should be kept in the muffin tins in the refrigerator until ready to serve. Makes 8 cups.

The Heritage House
This fashionable restaurant has had a reputation for fine dining that has been a tradition in the Cincinnati area since the turn of the century.

Cincinnati, Ohio
7664 Wooster Pike ~ Cincinnati, OH 45227 ~ 513-561-9300

235   *North Central Region*

Grand Marnier Cheesecake with Strawberries

Crust:
1¼ cups graham cracker crumbs
1 cup toasted pecans or hazelnuts
5 tablespoons butter, melted
2 tablespoons firmly packed light brown sugar
2 teaspoons grated orange peel

Filling:
4 8-ounce packages cream cheese, at room temperature
1 cup firmly packed light brown sugar
¼ cup Grand Marnier or other orange liqueur
¼ cup heavy cream
2 teaspoons vanilla
3 large eggs, room temperature, beaten to blend
2 large egg yolks

Position rack in center of oven and preheat to 350 degrees. Butter 9½-inch round spring form pan. Mix all crust ingredients in bowl. Press mixture firmly onto bottom and up sides of pan to within ½-inch of top edge. Bake 10 minutes. Maintain oven temperature. Transfer crust to rack and cool completely.

Using mixer, beat cream cheese in large bowl until very smooth. Beat in sugar, Grand Marnier, cream and vanilla. Add eggs and yolks and beat just until blended. Pour filling into prepared pan. Bake until the top puffs and is golden brown, about 50 minutes. Transfer to rack and cool 15 minutes (cake will fall as it cools). Maintain oven temperature.

Almond Torte

1   cup flour
1½   tablespoons sugar
¾   stick butter
2   egg yolks
1   cup heavy cream
1   cup sugar
¼   teaspoon salt
1   cup sliced almonds
¼   teaspoon almond extract

Combine flour, sugar and butter in food processor until like coarse meal. Add yolks and mix until combined. Press into 9-inch tart pan with removable bottom. Bake at 325 degrees for ten minutes.
For filling, combine cream, sugar and salt. Bring to boil over medium high heat, stirring frequently. Simmer over medium to medium low heat for five minutes, stirring occasionally. Add almonds and almond extract. Pour into crust and bake at 375 degrees for 25-30 minutes or until lightly browned on top. Serve with raspberry sauce.

Frozen Orange Custards

3   large egg yolks
½   cup cane sugar
1   teaspoon grated orange zest
1   cup heavy cream
½   teaspoon vanilla
2   generous tablespoons thawed orange juice concentrate

In a bowl, beat the egg yolks for 5 seconds. Add the sugar in small amounts. Beat the mixture until it is thick and pale. Add the orange zest.
In a separate bowl, beat the heavy cream until just blended. Add the orange concentrate and whipped cream to the yolk mixture and fold until blended. Divide the mixture into 1 cup molds or ramekins. Cover it with plastic wrap and freeze at least six hours.

Cranberry Cake with Hot Caramel Sauce

2   cups all-purpose flour
½   cups sugar
2   teaspoons baking powder
1½   tablespoons butter
3   cups cranberries, halved
1   cup milk

In a bowl, sift together flour, ½ cup sugar and baking powder. Add 4 teaspoons butter, cut into bits and combine the mixture until it resembles meal. Stir in the milk and cranberries. Line the bottom of a buttered 9-inch round cake pan with waxed paper. Butter and flour the paper. Pour the batter into pan and bake at 350 degrees for 45 minutes or until the sides of the cake pull slightly away from the pan. Cool cake in pan for 30 minutes, then turn it out onto a cooling rack. Remove wax paper and let cake cool completely.

Sauce: ½   cup firmly packed brown sugar
          ½   cup sugar
          ½   cup heavy cream
          2   tablespoons butter

In a saucepan, combine brown sugar, sugar, cream and butter. Bring to a boil over moderate heat while stirring constantly until sugar is dissolved. Serve the sauce with the cake.

The Inn at Cedar Falls
An outdoorsman's paradise, this inn is made up of several log cabins and breathtaking views.

Logan, Ohio
21190 St. ~ Logan, OH 43138 ~ 740-385-7489

The Inn at Honey Run

Ruth's Special Apple Pie

1	9-inch pastry shell
4	baking apples
⅔	cup sugar
¼	cup flour
⅛	teaspoon salt
1	cup sour cream
1	egg, beaten
1½	teaspoons vanilla extract
Topping:	½	cup flour
	⅓	cup firmly packed brown sugar
	⅓	cup sugar
	1	cup chopped walnuts
	¼	cup butter or margarine, softened

Preheat oven to 375 degrees. To prepare pastry, line a 9-inch pie pan with pastry; flute edges. Pare, core, and thinly slice apples; set aside. In large bowl, combine sugar, flour, salt, sour cream, egg, and vanilla. Stir well. Stir in apples. Pour into prepared pie shell. For crumb topping, mix all dry ingredients together. Cut in butter to make fine crumbs. Sprinkle crumbs evenly over top of pie. Bake for 20 minutes then reduce heat to 325 degrees and bake 30 to 35 minutes longer or until crumb topping is lightly browned. Cool on a wire rack. Cover and refrigerate to store.

The Inn at Honey Run

Located in the heart of the world's largest Amish population, this inn offers comfortable lodging and spectacular views.

Millersburg, Ohio

6920 County Rd. 203 ~ Millersburg, OH 44654-9018 ~ 330-674-0011

North Central Region

The Inn at Union Pier

Country Fruit Crisp

6   cups fresh fruit, peeled and sliced (pears, peaches, apples)
⅓   cup sugar
½   tablespoon lemon juice
½   teaspoon lemon peel, finely grated
1   cup quick cooking oats
⅓   cup brown sugar, firmly packed
2   tablespoons all-purpose flour
½   teaspoon ground cinnamon
½   teaspoon ground ginger
4   tablespoons butter

Preheat oven to 400 degrees. In a large bowl, toss fruit with sugar, lemon juice and lemon peel. Place 1 cup of fruit in each lightly greased ceramic boat. Combine oats, brown sugar, flour, cinnamon and ginger. Cut in butter with a fork or pastry blender until mixture is crumbly. Sprinkle over fruit.

Bake for 25-30 minutes, or until fruit is bubbling and topping is crisp. Hold in 175 degree oven, covered with foil.

John's Apple Pie

Pastry: 1⅓   cups all purpose flour
          1   4-ounce stick cold butter
          1   teaspoon salt (less if using salted butter)
          1   tablespoon sugar (optional)
          ¼   cup ice water

Combine dry ingredients in food processor bowl, cut butter in 2 or 3 pieces and process with mixing blade until mixed. With machine running slowly, pour ice water through feed tube. A ball of dough will form in 20-50 seconds.

Filling: 5-7 medium apples
          ¾-1 cup sugar
          2   tablespoons flour
          ⅛   teaspoon salt
          1   teaspoon cinnamon
          ¼   teaspoon nutmeg
          2   tablespoons butter

Peel, core and slice apples very thin. Mix sugar, flour, salt and spices. Place apples in crust, sprinkle with dry mixture and put butter on top, then top with crust. Bake at 400 degrees for 10 minutes, then reduce heat to 350 degrees for 40 minutes.

Amaretto Sour Cream Sauce

          3   cups sour cream
          ¾   cup brown sugar
          ⅛   cup amaretto

Mix together and serve over fresh fruit.

Chocolate Chip Cookies

32 ounces chocolate chips
5 cups flour
4 cups oatmeal (blend to powder)
3 cups chopped nuts
2 cups butter
2 cups sugar
2 cups brown sugar
4 eggs
2 teaspoons vanilla
1 teaspoon salt
2 teaspoons baking powder
2 teaspoons baking soda

Cream together butter and both sugars and then add in eggs and vanilla. In separate bowl mix together next 7 ingredients. Combine dry and wet mixtures and bake at 375 degrees for 8-10 minutes.

The Inn at Union Pier
Ideally located to enjoy Michigan's glorious four seasons.
Union Pier, Michigan
9708 Berrien ~ Union Pier, MI 49129 ~ 269-463-4700

Lydonville Mandarin Coconut Dessert

4   egg whites
¼   teaspoon cream of tartar
½   cup sugar
15 graham crackers crushed
1   cup chopped nuts
1   teaspoon vanilla
1   pint whipping cream
1   cup powdered sugar
1   3¾-ounce box instant pudding
¾   cup coconut
2   large cans mandarin oranges
    pinch of salt

Beat egg whites till stiff, not dry, adding salt, cream of tartar, and sugar. Fold in graham crackers and nuts, also vanilla. Bake at 325 degrees for 20-30 minutes in 8 x 8-inch greased pan. Cool.

Whip whipping cream and add powdered sugar and instant pudding. Mix well with beater. Add coconut. Stir in mandarin oranges. Spread on cool crust. Refrigerate 2-3 hours. Serve with toasted coconut and whipped cream.

Farm House Mud Pie

½ package chocolate wafers
½ cup butter, melted
1 quart coffee ice cream, softened
1 quart chocolate almond ice cream, softened
1 pint chocolate fudge sauce
   sliced almonds

Crush wafers and add butter. Mix well. Press into 9-inch pie plate. Cover with soft coffee ice cream. Put into freezer until firm. Top with chocolate-almond ice cream. Refreeze. Top with cold fudge sauce. Freeze for 10 hours. Top with whipped cream and sliced almonds. Serves 8-10.

The Inn on the Farm
This is a delightfully restored Victorian gentlemen's estate.
Brooklyn Center, Minnesota
6150 Summit Drive, N. ~ Brooklynn Center, MN 55430-2118

Old-Fashioned Maple Frango

¾　cup maple syrup
4　egg yolks
¼　cup alaga syrup
3　cups whipped cream

Warm syrup slightly before adding to warm egg yolks. Boil gently until thick. Cool. Whip cream and fold into maple mixture. Pour into pan three to four inches deep. Serves 8-10.

Lowell Inn
This inn has welcomed visitors with treasured traditions since 1930.

Stillwater, Minnesota
102 North Second St. ~ Stillwater, MN 55082 ~ 651-439-1100

Eileen Cookies

Cookie: 2   cups butter
          1   cup butter sifted flour
          2   tablespoons powdered sugar
          2   teaspoons vanilla

Mix all ingredients and form into small balls. Press down with a fork. Bake at 325-350 degrees for 8-10 minutes. Be careful not to overcook.

Frosting: 1   cup powdered sugar
            ⅛   pound butter
                  lemon juice to flavor

Mix all ingredients together, and spread between two cookies, once cooled. These make a delicious and delicate cookie.

Ludlow's Island Resort
An outdoorsman's paradise with eighteen guest cottages.

Cook, Minnesota
8166 Ludlow Dr. ~ P.O. Box 1146 ~ Cook, MN 55723 ~ 218-666-5407

Michillinda Beach Lodge

Michillinda Fruit Cocktail Torte

1   cup flour
1   cup sugar
1   teaspoon baking soda
1   egg
½   teaspoon salt
6   ounces fruit cocktail
⅔   cup chopped walnuts
3   teaspoons brown sugar

Blend flour, sugar, baking soda, and salt. Add eggs and fruit cocktail by hand. Pour into greased pan and sprinkle with brown sugar and chopped walnuts. Bake 30-45 minutes at 350 degrees.

Michillinda Beach Lodge
Guests return year after year to this family resort overlooking Lake Michigan.

Whitehall, Minnesota
5207 Scenic Dr. ~ Whitehall, MI 49461 ~ 231-893-1895

Montague Inn

Grand Marnier Mousse

3	tablespoons sugar
1	tablespoon water
3	egg whites
6	ounces white chocolate
½	teaspoon lemon juice
1	cup heavy cream
3	tablespoons Grand Marnier

Boil sugar in water to make a syrup (238 degrees on a candy thermometer). In a separate bowl, beat the egg whites until foamy. Pour the syrup in slowly and beat until stiff. Melt the chocolate in a double boiler. Add the lemon juice to the chocolate. Add the chocolate mixture to the egg whites.

Whip the heavy cream until soft peaks form. Add the liqueur. Fold the chocolate mixture into the whipped cream. Pour into stemmed glasses. Top with chunks of white chocolate. Refrigerate until ready to serve.

Dark chocolate may be substituted for white chocolate. Any liqueur may be substituted for the Grand Marnier.

Scones

⅔   cup butter or margarine, melted
⅓   cup milk
1   egg
1½   cups flour
1½   cups uncooked oats
¼   cup sugar
1   tablespoon baking powder
1   teaspoon cream of tartar
½   teaspoon salt
½   cup raisins or currants

Add melted butter, milk, and egg to combined dry ingredients; mix just until moistened. Stir in raisins. Drop by teaspoon onto a greased baking sheet. Bake at 425 degrees for 12-15 minutes or until a light golden brown.

Hazelnut Cheesecake

2¼   pounds cream cheese, room temperature
6   eggs
¾   cup toasted, chopped hazelnuts
¼   cup Frangelico (hazelnut liqueur)
1   tablespoon vanilla
½   tablespoon almond extract

Beat cream cheese until smooth. Add vanilla and almond extracts. Pour sugar in gradually. When completely mixed, add eggs, one at a time. Add hazelnuts. Pour mixture into a greased, 10-inch round cake pan, lined with parchment paper. Drizzle Frangelico over the mixture and stir in with a toothpick. Place pan in a water bath and bake at 450 degrees for 15 minutes. Lower the oven temperature to 300 degrees and bake for an additional hour, or until a knife inserted in the center comes out clean. Let cake cook completely and turn pan upside down on a cake plate. Peel parchment paper off. You may invert the cheesecake back onto another cake platter if you would like it top-side-up. Refrigerate until ready to serve. Top with whipped cream flavored with Frangelico.

Montague Inn
There are 18 guest rooms and warm hospitality at this inn.

Saginaw, Minnesota
1581 S Washington Ave. ~ Saginaw, MI 48601 ~ 989-752-3939

Nicollet Island Inn

Key Lime Pie

Filling   12   ounces cream cheese
              1½   14-ounce can condensed milk (21 ounces)
              1   tablespoon vanilla
              1   cup key lime juice
              1¼   tablespoons gelatin

Mix ingredients together and press into a greased, 9-inch cake pan. Bake for 10 minutes at 350 degrees.

Shell   2   cups graham cracker crumbs
              ¼   cup sugar
              ¼   cup melted butter

Dissolve the key lime juice and gelatin together.
Mix the cream cheese, condensed milk and vanilla; cream until smooth.
Once cheese and milk are smooth, add juice and gelatin and mix well.
Pour into the pre-baked shell.

Nicollet Island Inn
Overlooks the Mississippi River and dates back to 1893.

Minneapolis, Minnesota
95 Merriam St. ~ Minneapolis, MN 55401-1524 ~ 612-331-1800

Old Rittenhouse Inn

Strawberry Consommé

1	pint fresh strawberries
1⅔	cups freshly cut rhubarb
¾-1	cup sugar
½	cup soda water
1	3-inch cinnamon stick
2	cups water
½	cup burgundy wine
	sour cream

Set aside about six strawberries; cut up remaining berries and put in saucepan with rhubarb, cinnamon stick, sugar and water. Bring to a boil, reduce in heat and simmer until rhubarb is tender, about five minutes. Pour into strainer and press out juice (there should be three cups of rosy-pink juice). Add burgundy and soda. Slice remaining berries. Serve hot or chilled, garnished with sliced berries and dollops of sour cream. Serves 4 to 6.

Old Rittenhouse Inn

Built in 1890, this lovely Queen Anne style mansion with twenty-six guest rooms, serves elegant six-course dinners in the atmosphere of a Victorian dining room.

Bayfield, Wisconsin
P.O. Box 584 ~ Bayfield, WI 54814 ~ 715-779-5111

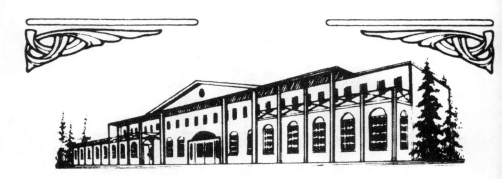

Pine Edge Inn

Caramel Walnut Pie

3   eggs
1   cup white syrup
½   teaspoon maple flavoring
¾   cup chopped walnuts
½   cup sugar
½   cup milk
1   9-inch pie crust
     whipped cream

Mix eggs, syrup, flavoring, sugar, and milk into regular unbaked pie crust. Sprinkle walnuts on top and bake 45 minutes at 350 degrees or until done. Cool. Serve topped with whipped cream.

Pine Edge Inn
It was here that Charles Lindbergh was honored with a glittering banquet in tribute to his historic flight in 1927.

Little Falls, Minnesota
308 First Street SE ~ Little Falls, MN 56345 ~ 612-632-6681

Sherwood Forest Bed and Breakfast

Vanilla Yogurt-Granola Dish

1	32-ounce Dannon Vanilla Yogurt
1	small box Kellogg's low-fat granola
½	pound dried cranberries, sweetened
½	pound apricots (dried)
1	kiwi
1	8-ounce can Dole pineapple chunks

Using an 8-ounce or 1-cup Pyrex bowl: Spoon in 4 to 5 ounces of vanilla yogurt. Sprinkle granola to cover yogurt. Sprinkle dried cranberries on top. Cut apricots in half and circle them around the middle (cut side in). Put a slice of kiwi in the middle. Put 4 chunks of pineapple in between apricots. Makes 10 individual dishes

Sherwood Forest Bed and Breakfast
Painted deep farmhouse red along the eastern shores of Lake Michigan, this inn offers a delightfully relaxed atmosphere.

Saugatuck, Michigan
938 Center St., P.O. Box 315 ~ Saugatuck, MI 49453 ~ 800-838-1246

Bay View Inn

Granny Smith Apple Pie

Filling:
- 2¼ pounds apples (peeled, cored and sliced)
- ¾ cup sugar
- ¼ cup cornstarch
- 1 teaspoon cinnamon

Topping:
- 1⅓ cups flour
- 5 ounces butter
- 7 ounces brown sugar

Combine sugar, corn starch and cinnamon. Mix with apples. Layer into pre-cooked pie shell. Sift flour, cut in butter and add to brown sugar. Sprinkle over pies. Yield: One pie.

Stafford's Bay View Inn
Listed on the National Register, this architectural beauty has played a rich part in the area since 1886.

Petoskey, Michigan
US 31 ~ North Petoskey, MI 49770 ~ 616-347-2771

Index of Recipes

Index

Index

Index of Inns

Northeast Region

Southeast Region

To order additional copies, make checks payable to:
Father & Son Publishing, Inc. and mail to:
4909 North Monroe Street • Tallahassee, Florida 32303

Please send me _____copies of *Sweet Memories: Desserts for Americas Favorite Inns*
@ $15.95 plus $3.00 each for postage and handling. Florida residents add 7.5% sales
tax.

Enclosed is my check or money order for $_____

Name _____

Address_____

City State _____Zip _____

Mastercard/Visa #_____ Exp. Date _____

— —

To order additional copies, make checks payable to:
Father & Son Publishing, Inc. and mail to:
4909 North Monroe Street • Tallahassee, Florida 32303

Please send me _____copies of *Sweet Memories: Desserts for Americas Favorite Inns*
@ $15.95 plus $3.00 each for postage and handling. Florida residents add 7.5% sales
tax.

Enclosed is my check or money order for $_____

Name _____

Address_____

City State _____Zip _____

Mastercard/Visa #_____ Exp. Date _____

— —

To order additional copies, make checks payable to:
Father & Son Publishing, Inc. and mail to:
4909 North Monroe Street • Tallahassee, Florida 32303

Please send me _____copies of *Sweet Memories: Desserts for Americas Favorite Inns*
@ $15.95 plus $3.00 each for postage and handling. Florida residents add 7.5% sales
tax.

Enclosed is my check or money order for $_____

Name _____

Address_____

City State _____Zip _____

Mastercard/Visa #_____ Exp. Date _____

Index

To order additional copies, make checks payable to:
Father & Son Publishing, Inc. and mail to:
4909 North Monroe Street • Tallahassee, Florida 32303

Please send me _____copies of *Sweet Memories: Desserts for Americas Favorite Inns*
@ $15.95 plus $3.00 each for postage and handling. Florida residents add 7.5% sales tax.

Enclosed is my check or money order for $_____

Name _____

Address_____

City State _____Zip _____

Mastercard/Visa #_____ Exp. Date _____

- -

To order additional copies, make checks payable to:
Father & Son Publishing, Inc. and mail to:
4909 North Monroe Street • Tallahassee, Florida 32303

Please send me _____copies of *Sweet Memories: Desserts for Americas Favorite Inns*
@ $15.95 plus $3.00 each for postage and handling. Florida residents add 7.5% sales tax.

Enclosed is my check or money order for $_____

Name _____

Address_____

City State _____Zip _____

Mastercard/Visa #_____ Exp. Date _____

- -

To order additional copies, make checks payable to:
Father & Son Publishing, Inc. and mail to:
4909 North Monroe Street • Tallahassee, Florida 32303

Please send me _____copies of *Sweet Memories: Desserts for Americas Favorite Inns*
@ $15.95 plus $3.00 each for postage and handling. Florida residents add 7.5% sales tax.

Enclosed is my check or money order for $_____

Name _____

Address_____

City State _____Zip _____

Mastercard/Visa #_____ Exp. Date _____